TABLE OF CONTENTS

                                                 Page

TABLE OF CONTENTS i

ACRONYMS iii

CHAPTER 1 INTRODUCTION 1

    Research Questions 2
    Increasingly Connected World 3
    U.S. Foreign Policy Pivot to Asia 6
    The Arab Spring and Lessons to be Learned 8
    North Korea and Nuclear Weapons 11
    A Korean Spring? 13
    Limitations 13
    Thesis Statement 14

CHAPTER 2 LITERATURE REVIEW 15

CHAPTER 3 RESEARCH METHODOLOGY 27

CHAPTER 4 ANALYSIS 32

    Geo-political Environment–"The Neighborhood".................... 32
        Egypt 32
        Libya 37
        Syria 40
        North Korea 43
        China 43
        South Korea 47
        United States 48
        Russia 50
        Japan 51
    Role of the Military (Security Forces) in Society 52
        Egypt 52
        Libya 55
        Syria 56
        North Korea 59

"The Network" 61
   Egypt 63
   Libya 65
   Syria 67
   North Korea 69

CHAPTER 5 CONCLUSIONS 75

   Themes 75

BIBLIOGRAPHY 84

ACRONYMS

FSA   Free Syrian Army

NATO   North Atlantic Treaty Organization

U.S.   United States

CHAPTER 1

INTRODUCTION

Fareed Zakaria recently highlighted a report regarding approximately 200 North Korean doctors, nurses and construction workers who were living and working in Libya during the anti-government uprising of 2011 and 2012. North Korean "Dear Leader" Kim Jong II originally sent these personnel to Libya in an effort to secure needed currency that could be sent back home. Now, although their money is still welcome in their North Korean homeland, the people are not because they witnessed the Libyan "Arab Spring" revolution. The closed and secretive state of North Korea will simply not allow any information from the world beyond its borders that might spark a similar revolution. Kim Jong II refused to allow the return of the citizens because they had witnessed the protests that resulted in the fall of Gaddafi. As Zakaria points out, "Editorials in South Korean newspapers say that only 1 percent of North Koreans have even heard of the Arab Spring."[1]

Kim Jong II, the leader of the Democratic People's Republic of Korea (commonly, and hereafter, referred to as North Korea) died on December 17, 2011. Kim Jong II had continued the isolation policies that his father Kim II Sung had established prior to his death in 1994 resulting in North Korea's seclusion from the international community. The Soviet Union appointed Kim II Sung the leader of North Korea following the partitioning of Korea at the end of World War II. Now, following Kim Jong

---

[1]Fareed Zakaria, "Will North Koreans Rise Up?" *CNN*, November 14, 2011, http://globalpublicsquare.blogs.cnn.com/2011/11/14/zakaria-will-the-north-koreans-rise-up/ (accessed December 12, 2011).

II's death, his youngest son Kim Jong Un appears to have taken over as the "Great Successor" and leader of North Korea. The world does not know much about the new leader in North Korea, but Kim Jong Un takes over during a very turbulent time in the world for oppressive regimes.

Following popular revolutions in Egypt, Tunisia, Libya, and Yemen, long established regimes have fallen, removing dictators throughout the Middle East and North Africa. Autocratic leaders all over the world have taken note of the events that led to these revolutions and the conditions that perpetuated their success. Even now, the leadership in Syria is trying desperately to prevent the collapse of President Bashar al-Assad's regime. At the same time, the autocratic Saudi Arabian regime, which *The Economist* described as "the Arab counter-revolution's engine,"[2] has taken steps to eradicate the seeds of dissatisfaction among its people by reportedly promising $30 billion in aid for the unemployed and the poor and raising salaries for government employees, particularly the military.[3]

Research Questions

Against the backdrop of successful revolutions and regimes desperately trying to retain their hold on power, the primary research question that this analysis seeks to examine is whether the conditions that existed during the Arab Spring exist in North Korea and to what degree is a "Korean Spring" possible in the communist state. If the

---

[2]*The Economist*, "The King's Sad Men," May 5, 2012, http://www.economist.com/node/21554229 (accessed April 2012), 48.

[3]Nawaf Obaid, "There Will Be No Uprising in Saudi Arabia," *Foreign Policy*, March 10, 2011, http://www.foreignpolicy.com/articles/2011/03/10/there_will_be_ no_uprising_in_saudi_arabia (accessed December 13, 2011).

study indicates that a Korean Spring in the style of the Arab Spring is unlikely, does a revolutionary model exist that could potentially propose how a popular revolution could occur in North Korea?

Increasingly Connected World

Due to the increasing interconnectedness of our globalized world, events that happen in the Middle East and North Africa have greater global impact than ever before. *New York Times* columnist, Thomas Friedman, who has written extensively about globalization in the twenty-first century recently noted that because of modern social networking tools such as Facebook and Twitter "the world has gone from connected to hyper-connected."[4] Instability in other parts of the globe therefore impacts the lives of Americans in a much more direct and instantaneous manner. In 2003, James Lindsay wrote in the *Brookings Review* that globalization was a challenge across the full spectrum of governmental and private endeavors such as politics, economics, and security.[5] Lindsay's argument suggests that as the world becomes more connected, events in Egypt and Libya will have immediate consequences for America's security, economy, and overall vital interests. To support its own national interests, the United States (U.S.) of America must position itself to understand and, if possible influence the outcomes of these and future uprisings.

---

[4]Thomas Friedman, "A Theory of Everything (sort Of)," *New York Times*, August 13, 2011, http://www.nytimes.com/2011/08/14/opinion/sunday/Friedman-a-theory-of-everyting-sort-of.html (accessed December 18, 2011).

[5]James M. Lindsay, "The Globalization of Politics: American Foreign Policy For a New Century," *Brookings Review* (Winter 2003), http://www.cfr.org/world/globalization-politics-american-foreign-policy-new-century/p6330 (accessed May 18, 2012).

On June 4, 2009, before the start of the Arab Spring, President Barack Obama gave a speech in Cairo, Egypt that many believed would change the relationship between the U.S. and the Muslim world. Much of the President's remarks focused on the usual foreign policy topics such as Islamic violent extremism, the Israeli-Palestinian conflict, and nuclear proliferation. Late in his speech, however, the President addressed the topic of democracy in the Middle East, saying:

> America does not presume to know what is best for everyone, just as we would not presume to pick the outcome of a peaceful election. But I do have an unyielding belief that all people yearn for certain things: the ability to speak your mind and have a say in how you are governed; confidence in the rule of law and the equal administration of justice; government that is transparent and doesn't steal from the people; the freedom to live as you choose. These are not just American ideas; they are human rights. And that is why we will support them everywhere.[6]

These remarks suggested American support of real democracy in the Middle East even though the U.S. had previously supported repressive oligarchies in places such as Saudi Arabia, Kuwait, and Qatar.

Despite President Obama's pledge, some have argued the U.S. government did little to operationalize that promise during the early Arab Spring uprisings. For example, in an article published in *Foreign Policy*, Eric Patterson questioned what steps the Obama administration had taken to support this view and argued that not much had been done. Troublingly, he concluded that the President and his foreign policy team seemed to have been "caught totally off-guard by events in the region," noting that "many embassies

---

[6]The White House, Remarks by The President (Barack Obama) "On a New Beginning," Press Release (Cairo, Egypt, 2009), 1.

were on their own to respond."[7] Jeremy Salt, in *Interface Journal*, charges that governments, more so than other institutions, should have been more aware of what was developing in the Middle East because that is exactly the task of their intelligence services."[8]

When Libyan rebel groups attempted to oust dictator Moammar Gaddafi from power, the Obama administration changed course by providing military capabilities, in conjunction with North Atlantic Treaty Organization (NATO) countries to assist rebel groups in eventually finding and killing Gaddafi. At the time, France, Great Britain, and the U.S. felt that intervention was required because of the humanitarian crisis that was occurring. Additionally, France and Great Britain felt that chaos in Libya would directly and adversely impact their interests.

Sudden regime change in North Korea would likely have similar direct effects on the U.S. and its interests. Instability following a collapse of Kim Jong Un's regime could potentially cause friction with China and threaten long-term allies Japan and South Korea. If the U.S. were to be caught off-guard in Asia, as it was during the early days of the Arab Spring, the American interests could be seriously threatened. Therefore, it is important that the U.S. government recognize and prepare for the possibility of an anti-government revolution in North Korea.

---

[7]Eric Patterson, "The Arab Spring vs. Cairo," *Foreign Policy Journal* (November 4, 2011), http://www.foreignpolicyjournal.com/2011/11/04/the-arab-spring-vs-cairo/ (accessed December 8, 2011).

[8]Jeremy Salt, "Containing the "Arab Spring," *Interface Journal* (May 2012): 54-66, http://www.interfacejournal.net/wordpress/wp-content/uploads/2012/05/Interface-4-1-Salt.pdf (accessed May 18, 2012).

U.S. Foreign Policy Pivot to Asia

The increased economic opportunities in Asia coupled with the rising Chinese power in the region are important reasons that the U.S. must recognize it has a vested interest in the future of the Korean Peninsula. As Asian economies continue to outpace those of Europe, the U.S. and its security will become increasingly tied to events in the region. On January 12, 2011, Secretary of State Hillary Rodham Clinton outlined America's future strategy and emphasized that the futures of America and Asia are intertwined.[9] Indeed, economic indications are that Asian economies are performing better than the economies of the European Union. According to the International Monetary Fund, the world's second, third, tenth and fifteenth largest economies reside in Asia and as an International Monetary Fund report dated April 2011 states, "[e]ven though growth has moderated from cyclical highs to more sustainable rates, Asia continues to outpace other regions."[10] Moreover, a 2011 International Monetary Fund forecast predicts that "China's economy will surpass that of America in real terms in 2016."[11] China's economic rise is one of the main reasons why American foreign policy is shifting from the Middle East to Asia.

---

[9]East-West Center, "Clinton: America's Future Linked to Future of Asia Pacific Region," http://www.eastwestcenter.org/news-center/east-west-wire/clinton-americas-future-linked-to-future-of-asia-pacific-region (accessed December 17, 2011).

[10]International Monetary Fund, *World Economic Outlook 2011* (Washington, DC: IMF Multimedia Services Division, 2011), 90.

[11]Brett Arends, "IMF Bombshell: Age of America Nears End," *Wall Street Journal,* April 25, 2011, http://www.marketwatch.com/story/imf-bombshell-age-of-america-about-to-end-2011-04-25 (accessed December 20, 2011).

Recognizing these factors and their impact on both the economy of the U.S. and its security, Secretary of Defense Leon Panetta wrote in the 2012 *National Defense Strategy*:

> Accordingly, while the U.S. military will continue to contribute to security globally, we will of necessity rebalance toward the Asia-Pacific region. Our relationships with Asian allies and key partners are critical to the future stability and growth of the region. We will emphasize our existing alliances, which provide a vital foundation for Asia-Pacific security.[12]

Therefore, the U.S. must maintain a strong presence in Asia not only for economic purposes but also for national security. Although the U.S. has strong allies in South Korea, Japan, the Philippines, Australia and New Zealand, it also has a strong challenger in China. In fact, in a 2011 report, the Department of Defense warned that China possesses new weapon systems that threaten the 'regional military balances' that currently exist in Asia.[13] The growth of China could potentially threaten security in the region as its military becomes more capable and expands its sphere of influence throughout Asia.

In a show of reassurance to friendly governments in the Asian-Pacific region and a response to Chinese expansion, the U.S. recently announced an agreement with Australia to station U.S. Marines there. Such a move suggests that the U.S. recognizes that activities in Asia could have as much impact on the U.S. and its people as the events in the Middle East have had throughout much of the 20th century. Additionally, this

---

[12]Department of Defense, *Sustaining U.S. Global Leadership: Priorities for 21st Century Defense* (Washington, DC: Government Printing Office, 2012), 2.

[13]Lolita Bolder, "Pentagon Worries Over Chinese Military's Rapid Growth," *Associated Press*, August 25, 2011, http://www.military.com/news/article/pentagon-worries-over-chinese-militarys-rapid-growth.html (accessed December 20, 2011).

move serves a concrete example of the "re-balancing" towards Asia that Panetta outlined in the *National Security Strategy* in 2012.

The Arab Spring and Lessons to be Learned

In December 2010, the Arab Spring began in Tunisia in the city of Sidi Bouzid after the police seized a vegetable cart owned by Mohammed Bouazizi. Bouazizi, a local street vendor, self-immolated in front of a Tunisian police headquarters after the police seized his cart. Media coverage of this incident sparked daily protests in Sidi Bouzid, which quickly spread to the capital city of Tunis. The protests in Tunis eventually led Tunisian President Zine al-Abidine Ben Al to step down from office. The Tunisian uprising was the first modern Arab revolution to succeed in removing a long serving autocrat that would come to define the Arab Spring.

From Tunisia, revolutionary enthusiasm spread to Egypt, where thousands of young Egyptian protesters camped in Tahir Square in downtown Cairo demanding changes in a government that had failed to cope with deteriorating economic conditions. Ultimately these uprisings helped to force Hosni Mubarak from power. While localized violence took place early in the uprising, the Egyptian military did not intervene on behalf of the government, tacitly allowing the protests to occur. Much of the success in overthrowing Hosni Mubarak flowed from the protestors' refusal to leave Tahir Square combined with the Egyptian military's passive approval of the protests.

After Mubarak's removal, Egypt held its first truly democratic elections. The Muslim Brotherhood, which historically had been an Islamist political organization, together with the Salafist Al Nour Party, received 65 percent of the seats in the Egyptian Parliament–handily beating secular and more moderate candidates. These results, while democratic, cannot be viewed by the U.S. government as immense progress in the Middle East.[14] Whether by choice or by circumstance, the U.S. is on the sidelines in parts of the Arab world and has been left to watch while political parties with historically Islamic agendas have won democratic elections. Nonetheless, the U.S. government has engaged the Muslim Brotherhood because the political party has emerged as one of the leading players in the post-Mubarak Egyptian politics. There is hope that the Muslim Brotherhood is a reformed organization that is becoming involved in Egyptian politics to make a difference for the better. Given the Brotherhood's long-time goal of implementing Sharia Law throughout the Arab world, the U.S. should be wary.

Based on the success in Cairo, uprisings soon took place in Yemen and Bahrain. Unlike in Egypt, however, protesters in those nations were met with a strong military response. Bahrain received military assistance in the form of troops from Saudi Arabia to suppress the uprisings. Saudi Arabia supported its Sunni-led neighbors against the predominantly Shiite demonstrators to prevent demonstrations from crossing into Saudi Arabia.

The most violent uprising, however, occurred in Libya. Rebel groups in the eastern Libyan city of Misrata started an armed resistance against the Gaddafi regime. Over the course of nine months, rebel groups backed by NATO air power fought to the capital city of Tripoli. In contrast to the passive response of the Egyptian military, almost constant battles occurred between Gaddafi's military loyalists and anti-government rebel militias, plunging Libya into civil war. On October 20, 2011 rebel forces captured and killed Libya's dictator, Moammar Gaddafi. Since then, rival militias continue to compete

---

[14]Friedman, "Watching Elephants Fly."

for control of Libya. Recently, the leader of the Transitional National Council Mustafa Abdel Jalil warned that the competing militias could drag Libya deeper into a more enduring civil war.[15]

The longest and most difficult revolution thus far has occurred in Syria. The Syrian uprising has not produced the quick resolution that occurred in Egypt for a number of reasons. First, the Syrian military has taken an active role in quelling the uprisings, and has killed scores of Syrian protesters in the 10 months since uprisings began. Second, anti-government opposition groups' organization has been less successful than were the anti-government group in Libya. Some Syrian military personnel have joined the resistance, but these defections have had little effect. According to journalist Alastair Beach, the Free Syrian Army (FSA) is large enough to engage in a protracted struggle, but too small to overthrow the Syrian regime. The size of the FSA is estimated to be between 10,000 and 40,000 fighters.[16]

It is important to note that each individual revolution that comprised the Arab Spring had unique characteristics. While it is possible, in retrospect, to view the Arab Spring as a natural progression from country to country, fed by media outlets broadcasting the dramatic images of revolution, the circumstances leading to each revolution and the methods used by the protesters in situation differed in subtle yet

---

[15]Mahmoud Habbous and Ali Shuaib, "Militias May Drag Libya Into Civil War, Transitional Government Chief Says," *Washington Post*, January 4, 2012, http://www.washingtonpost.com/world/update-1-militias-may-drag-libya-into-civil-war-ntc-chief/2012/01/04/gIQAO8kebP_story.html (accessed January 7, 2012).

[16]Alastair Beach, "Assad Offers an Amnesty to the 'criminals' of the Syrian Uprising," *The Independent*, http://www.independent.co.uk/news/world/middle-east/assad-offers-an-amnesty-to-the-criminals-of-the-syrian-uprising-6290176.html (accessed December 15, 2011).

distinct ways. Lisa Anderson, President of the American University in Cairo, summarized

the importance for the U.S. of understanding the nuances of instability in the May 2011

edition of *Foreign Affairs*, where she stated that:

> As a result [of the Arab Spring], Tunisia, Egypt, and Libya face vastly different
> challenges moving forward. Tunisians will need to grapple with the class
> divisions manifesting themselves in the country's continuing political unrest.
> Egyptians must redesign their institutions of government. And Libyans will need
> to recover from a bloody civil war. For the United States to fulfill its goals in the
> region, it will need to understand these distinctions and distance itself from the
> idea that the Tunisian, Egyptian, and Libyan uprisings constitute a cohesive Arab
> revolt.[17]

The U.S. government does not want China's influence on the Korean Peninsula to

produce a substantial power shift resembling what is occurring in parts of the Middle

East, but must nonetheless confront this possibility to ensure the protection of its

interests. The many paths to revolution that occurred in the Arab Spring, however, make

clear that in preparing for any such potential situation, the U.S must plan for all scenarios

in the event of a sudden change in the government of North Korea. This is especially true

with so much at stake in Asia both economically and with respect to U.S. security.

Therefore, with respect to planning for any future instability in Asia, the U.S. must

prepare for all contingencies.

North Korea and Nuclear Weapons

North Korea holds one asset thus far absent throughout the Arab revolutions in

the Arab world–nuclear weapons. The ballistic missiles and nuclear weapons on the

Korean Peninsula have been in the forefront of U.S. foreign policy in Asia for much of

---

[17]Lisa Anderson, "Demystifying the Arab Spring," *Foreign Affairs* (May/June 2011), http://www.foreignaffairs.com/articles/67693/lisa-anderson/demystifying-the-arab-spring (accessed December 7, 2011).

the last two decades. Throughout much of the 1990s, Kim Jong II used the nuclear dispute to gain concessions on the parts of the U.S., South Korea, and Japan, culminating in the signing of the Agreed Framework in 1994, wherein North Korea agreed to halt its enrichment of uranium in exchange for American food and fuel shipments.

In 2003, North Korea again abandoned the nuclear Non-Proliferation Treaty. The regime claimed to be responding to threats levied by the U.S. government, a common accusation used to justify its actions. Since the 1990s, North Korea's 'nuclear extortion' has generated approximately $6 billion in aid from the U.S. South Korea, China, and Japan.[18] This extortion program reached a new level when North Korea successfully tested a nuclear device in October 2006, while boycotting the "six-party" talks. In addition to North Korea, these included South Korea, Japan, China, Russia, and the U.S.[19]

Prior to the death of Kim Jong II, a rejuvenation of the six-party talks appeared possible. However, the leader's death has, temporarily at least, halted that possibility. Robert Gallucci, who served as the chief U.S. nuclear negotiator during the 1994 that produced in the Agreed Framework said recently, "During the transition [North Korean leadership], anything is possible. Dramatic change is bad and under that . . . we have a new leader who may want to demonstrate his chops domestically and internationally and

---

[18]Daniel Bynum and Jennifer Lind, "Pyongyang's Survival Strategy: Tools of Authoritarian Control in North Korea," *Harvard Belfer Center* (June 2010): 65, abstract in *International Security* 35, no. 1 (Summer 2010): 44-74.

[19]Amy Zalman, "Timeline of North Korea's Nuclear Weapons Program," About.com, http://terrorism.about.com/od/usforeignpolicy/a/NorthKorea.htm (accessed January 8, 2011).

do dramatic things that would not be good."[20] The transfer of power from Kim Jong II to Kim Jong Un creates a high level of uncertainty in the international community.

A Korean Spring?

Set against the backdrop of the current international uncertainty and Middle Eastern revolt, this research thesis addresses the likelihood of a popular revolution taking place in North Korea, a nation that has undergone its own radical change with the recent death of Kim Jong II and the rise to power of his youngest son. This thesis therefore analyzes the conditions that led to the Arab Spring and applies that analysis to the current situation in North Korea to assess the possibility of a similar popular uprising occurring in North Korea.

Limitations

The major limiting factor in the research thesis is the current nature of the topic. The Arab Spring has just had its one-year anniversary, so one cannot say with precision what lies ahead for the Middle Eastern region and what effect these revolutions will have on future events. Democratic elections have taken place in Egypt, but the country still does not have an elected president. Libya is mired in a situation of feuding rebel groups who are competing for power. The situation in Syria is in its infancy with no end in sight and no sign that the Assad regime will cede power.

---

[20]Suzanne Kelly and Pam Benson, "North Korea's Nuclear Program," *CNN*, December 20, 2011, http://security.blogs.cnn.com/2011/12/20/north-koreas-nuclear-program/ (accessed January 8, 2011).

Thesis Statement

Based on the analysis of the Arab Spring revolutions in Egypt, Libya, and Syria and comparing those conditions to the environment in North Korea, it is unlikely that a Korean Spring will occur in North Korea.

CHAPTER 2

LITERATURE REVIEW

American leaders have predicted the imminent collapse of the North Korean regime numerous times. In 1996, General Gary Luck, then-Commander of U.S. forces in Korea, declared during testimony before the House Armed Services Committee that "The question is not will this country [North Korea] disintegrate, but rather how it will disintegrate, by implosion or explosion, and when."[21] In 2000, "Director of Central Intelligence George Tenet warned that 'sudden, radical and possibly dangerous change remains a real possibility in North Korea, and that change could come at any time'."[22] Similarly, in 2003, the U.S. Deputy Secretary of Defense Paul Wolfowitz "said that North Korea was 'teetering on the edge of economic collapse'."[23] To date, each of these predictions has proven false. Indeed, the Kim Jong II regime even survived a devastating famine throughout the country in the mid-1990s, during which the North Korean people launched no large civil protests for economic change or government aid. Andrei Lankov wrote about the famine, "North Korea's starving farmers did not rebel. They just died."[24]

Many works have examined the future of the Korean Peninsula, covering scenarios ranging from non-conflict to full-scale war. An abundance of books, papers,

---

[21]Selig S. Harrison, *Korean Endgame: A Strategy For Reunification and U.S. Disengagement* (Princeton, NJ: Princeton University Press, 2002), 3.

[22]Bynum and Lind, 44.

[23]Ibid.

[24]Andrei Lankov, "Staying Alive: Why North Korea Will Not Change," *Foreign Affairs* 87, no. 2 (March/April 2008): 15.

and articles use the word "reunification" in their title or have the idea central to their theses. The reunification models center on three types of scenarios in order of increasing degrees of conflict: (1) the "no landing"; (2) the "soft landing"; and (3) the "hard landing." Although few, if any, reunification scenarios identify a popular civil uprising as one of the likely catalysts, a review of the pre-2011 analysis is nonetheless relevant to the study of the effects of an internal uprising on North Korea.

In 1999, the Rand Corporation conducted an extensive study titled "Preparing for Korean Reunification: Scenarios and Implications." In the study, author Jonathan D. Pollack identifies three widely accepted outcomes for North Korea based on steps they could undertake. The first possibility is the "no landing" scenario. Pollack defines this scenario as "The maintenance of the status quo, where the regime is able to muddle through without enacting any major economic reforms, and with no major concessions in relations with the [Republic of Korea (South Korea)]." This scenario assumes continuing Chinese support to the regime, including food subsidies, and that the North Korean military remains loyal to the leadership despite the uncertainty of a transitional period.[25]

The second Rand scenario is the "soft landing." Pollack defines this scenario as "A process whereby gradual and controlled implementation of selective economic reforms enables a command economy to assume some characteristics of a market economy, although no regime change occurs." In this scenario, the regime remains in power, but makes some much needed, if limited, changes to open the economy to the

---

[25]Jonathan Pollack and Chung Min Lee, *Preparing For Korean Unification: Scenarios and Implications* (Santa Monica, CA: RAND Corporation, 1999), 41, http://www.rand.org/pubs/monograph_reports/2007/MR1040.pdf (accessed January 28, 2011).

international system. In 1991, Kim II Sung undertook economic reform by creating the Rajin-Sonbong special economic zone for free trade to entice foreign investment in North Korea. However, in the less than 10 years the zone lost its status amid reports of corruption by North Korean leaders in that region.[26] Under Kim Jong II, North Korea attempted currency reform in 2010, which resulted in a loss of purchasing power for most North Koreans combined with out of control inflation. None of these attempted reforms truly transformed the North Korean economy in any meaningful way.[27]

The final scenario outlined in the study is termed the "hard landing." It is defined as "The inability of the regime in power to maintain effective political, economic, social and military control, ultimately leading to the dissolution of the regime and in the extreme case, the state." The "hard landing" scenario is the most dangerous and has the largest spectrum of possible outcomes. It also presents the largest opportunity for chaos in Northeast Asia. The Rand study warns that such a scenario "could precipitate internal violence in the North or military operations against the South, up to and including large scale war launched in desperation."[28]

Another possible model (that seems implausible at this point) is that North Korea would willingly move to reunite with South Korea and, accordingly, open dialogue with the U.S. North Korea signaled the possibility of this approach in 1972, when representatives of North and South Korea met to discuss future engagement. The result of

---

[26]John Kim and Andray Abrahamian, "Why World Should Watch Rason," The Diplomat Blogs, entry posted December 22, 2011, http://the-diplomat.com/new-leaders-forum/2011/12/22/why-world-should-watch-rason/ (accessed May 20, 2012).

[27]Pollack and Lee, 40.

[28]Ibid.

this overture by North Korea was the Joint Communique of North-South Dialogue, which

stated that:

> The principles are (1) reunification should be achieved through independent
> Korea effort without being subject to external imposition or interference, (2)
> peaceful means without the use of force against each other, and (3) a greater
> national unity transcending difference in ideas, ideologies, and systems.[29]

However, the joint statement became obsolete two years later when the Democratic

People's Republic of Korea proposed direct talks with the U.S. to decrease tension on the

Korean Peninsula. The refusal to direct dialogue with South Korea emphasized the fact

that Pyongyang did not recognize the Republic of Korea as a sovereign nation. The

proposed talks with the Americans, which violated most of the objectives outlined in the

Joint Communique, aspired to complicate the U.S.-South Korean relationship.[30] Direct

talks never materialized and the U.S. presence in South Korea has endured.

There have been some additional initiatives in this direction, such as the joint

Kaesong Industrial Park, North-South family reunions, and South Korea's "Sunshine

Policy." However, 40 years after the issuance of the Joint Communique, obstacles exist

that were not present at that time that it was prepared. For example, in 1972, both sides of

the Korean peninsula were less than 20 years removed from fighting the Korean War.

Neither side had experienced much economic vitality, and therefore both sides were

likely to be open to reducing hostilities and leaving open the door for reunification. Since

---

[29]Young Whan Kihl, "South Korea's Unification Policy in the 1980s," in *Korean Unification: New Perspectives and Approaches*, ed. Tae-Hwan Kwak (Seoul: Kyungnam University Press, 1984), 24.

[30]James L. Schoff and Yaron Eisenberg, *Peace Regime Building On the Korean Peninsula: What's Next?* (Cambridge, MA: Institute for Foreign Policy Affairs, May 2009), 12.

that point, the economic fate of the two nations has moved in opposite directions. South Korea's economic "miracle growth" began following trade reform policies in the 1960s which lowered tariffs on imports and negotiated similar concessions on their exports to Japan and the U.S.[31] Improving trade practices culminated in the U.S.-South Korea Free Trade Agreement, which was ratified by both governments in 2011. These factors suggest that South Korea's economy has grown exponentially because of openness to foreign trade, while North Korea's economy is fatally flawed because of its isolationist policies. Furthermore, South Korea and the U.S. have strengthened their alliance. Future decisions are likely to be a joint endeavor between the two nations. Similarly, China has continued its support for North Korea, suggesting its involvement in any voluntary unification decisions. Despite these complications, optimism about re-unification does exist in South Korea, as illustrated by the Unification Ministry, the head of which is a cabinet position.

Works that address North and South Korean relations often view the situation on the Korean Peninsula through the prism of the relationship between East and West Germany in the latter half of the 20th century. In one such work, Robert Kelly, a professor at Busan University, wrote an article in The Korean Journal of Defense Analysis in December 2011 discussing the relevance of East and West German reconciliation and its application for possible Korean reunification. In the argument for reunification he writes, "Both sides believe the 'two states one people' outcome is

---

[31]Michelle Connolly and Kei-Mu Yi, *How Much of South Korea's Growth Miracle Can Be Explained by Trade Policy?* (San Francisco, CA: Federal Reserve Bank of San Francisco, September, 2008), 27, http://www.frbsf.org/publications/economics/papers/2008/wp08-23bk.pdf (accessed May 20, 2012).

temporary."[32] Kelly notes that unlike the tribal societies of the Middle East, Korean and German societies are one-ethnic cultures. This claim is supported by the experience of Condoleezza Rice who, in a 2010 interview, recalled being in Germany in the weeks leading up to the fall of the Berlin Wall. Rice remembers "all of a sudden, this conference was now Germans talking to Germans about the prospects for Germany moving forward, and you could just feel in the air that something fundamental had changed. This was about three weeks before the fall of the wall."[33] However, Dr. Kelly's thesis is that East-West German reunification is unlikely to occur on the Korean Peninsula: "The balance of forces [i.e. China versus the U.S., South Korea] favors a more politicized, more expensive, and more internationally contested Korean reunification course than in Germany."[34]

One of the leading scholars on North Korean society is Andrei Lankov, a Russian born professor at Kookmin University in Seoul and an adjunct professor of East Asian studies at the Australian National University. In November, 2011 he wrote an article in the *Asia Times* titled, "Conditions Unripe for North Korean Revolt" that studied the likelihood of a revolution similar to the Arab Spring occurring in North Korea. Lankov asserts that revolutions occur because of two major factors. First, peoples' led uprisings are not generally engineered by members of the lowest class of society. Revolutions

---

[32]Robert Kelly, "The German-Korean Unification Parallel," *The Korean Journal of Defense Analysis* 23, no. 4 (December 2011): 461, http://www.kida.re.kr/data/kjda/ 02_Robert%20Kelly.pdf (accessed January 2012).

[33]Interview, Condoleezza Rice: On German Reunification, Spiegel Online International, September 29, 2010, http://www.spiegel.de/international/world/ 0,1518,719444,00.html (accessed January 2012).

[34]Kelly, 457.

throughout Eastern Europe and Russia were organized and led by members of the "intellectual circles." North Korea has created a society where those "circles" cannot form to share and ferment new ideas. Secondly, Lankov states, "People start revolutions when they know alternatives to the current system, when they believe things might and should be better." He argues that prior to the Arab Spring the people of Tunisia and Egypt lived far more comfortable lifestyles than the average North Korean.[35] It should be noted that this article was written prior to the death of Kim Jong II. However, the lack of access to external information and the absence of true opposition groups to the regime that Lankov cites as the major obstacles to an Arab Spring-type uprising are equally true under Kim Jong Un.

Fareed Zakaria agrees that the modern tools of revolution, such as cell phones and internet access are not present in North Korea. Zakaria estimates that only 1.5 percent of all North Koreans has access to cell phones. The unavailability of these devices limit the possibility that discontent could spread quickly similar to what occurred in Egypt. Zakaria further notes that China–the only supporter of the North Korean regime–is unlikely to encourage revolt because, "there is little appetite in China, the one country with influence in North Korea, to force change in Pyongyang."[36]

Indeed, it appears that the North Korean regime already has taken steps to prevent an Arab Spring-style revolt from taking hold on the peninsula. Adrian Hong, who created the non-profit organization Liberty in North Korea, believes that the North Korean

---

[35]Andrei Lankov, "Conditions Unripe For North Korea Revolt," *Asia Times*, November 17, 2011, http://atimes.com/atimes/Korea/MK17Dg01.html (accessed December 2011).

[36]Zakaria, "Will the North Koreans revolt?"

regime has paid close attention to the situation in the Middle East and reported that, "amidst the spread of the Arab Spring, North Korea reportedly moved tanks, barricades, and military units to pre-positioned locations in Pyongyang, just in case."[37] The *China Post* reported that North Korea has put severe travel restrictions on foreigners and cancelled the daily flight to Kuwait by its major airline, Air Koryo. These moves are almost assuredly to restrict information about the revolutions inside North Korea.[38]

The death of the "Dear Leader" has led to a split among academics regarding North Korea's future. Brian Reynolds Myers, an international studies professor at Dongseo University in Korea believes that the transition has proceeded exactly as choreographed prior to Kim Jong II's death. He argues that the West is incorrectly predicting internal instability because of Kim Jong Un's age or inexperience. Myers writes "in any case, the notion that army generals or any other important faction would object to Kim Jong-Un's takeover was an improbable one to begin with; no North Korean could oppose the hereditary succession without being opposed to the state itself."[39]

Myers does believe that the regime must continue to show the people that it has their well-being at the center of its policies, arguing that "though Kim Jong Un appears secure inside the elite, the state as a whole must continue showing the masses that it is

[37]Adrian Hong, "How to Free North Koreans," *Foreign Policy*, December 19, 2011, http://www.foreignpolicy.com/articles/2011/12/19/how_to_free_north_korea?page=0,3 (accessed January 2012).

[38]"Arab Spring Makes North Korea Nervous," *China Post*, November 13, 2011, http://www.chinapost.com.tw/commentary/the-china-post/special-to-the-china-post/2011/11/13/322766/Arab-Spring.htm (accessed May 20, 2012).

[39]B. R. Myers, "Dynasty, North Korean-Style," *New York Times*, January 7, 2012, http://www.nytimes.com/2012/01/08/opinion/sunday/dynasty-north-korean-style.html?_r=1 (accessed January 2012).

worthy of its beloved founder."[40] That task is made much easier by the fact that the North

Korean government controls most messages through state-run media outlets.

One scholar disagrees with Myers' assessment of the transfer of power to Kim

Jong Un. Victor Cha, a professor at Georgetown University and Senior Adviser at the

Center for Strategic and International Studies writes, "It would be wrong to interpret from

the funeral proceedings that all in Pyongyang is back to normal."[41] Cha believes that

downfalls of similar types of communist or autocratic regimes are preceded by an

increasing crack down on their subjects. North Korean leaders have resisted real reform

and thus will only increase repression of their people if they feel threatened. He terms this

"neo-Juche conservatism."[42] Cha believes that the Arab Spring is one of those events that

will contribute to a more hardline approach. Cha surmises, "This system cannot hold, and

we should all be ready when the moment of truth for this dictatorship arrives."[43]

While Cha suggests that eventual regime collapse is likely in North Korea,

Thomas Friedman believes the same was true for the Arab Spring. Friedman, arguably

the most prominent analyst of the ongoing situation in the Middle East and North Africa

writes, "I still believe this Arab democracy movement was inevitable, necessary and built

---

[40]Ibid.

[41]Victor Cha, "North Korea's Moment of Truth, *CNN*, December 27, 2011, http://globalpublicsquare.blogs.cnn.com/2011/12/27/cha-north-koreas-moment-of-truth/ (accessed December 2011).

[42]Ibid.

[43]Ibid.

on a deep and authentic human quest for freedom, dignity and justice."[44] However, he argues that not every nation's situation is the same and warns that outcomes could differ substantially, an important consideration in determining the likelihood of a North Korean revolt.

The greatest difficulty in outlining what has been written about the Arab Spring is the sheer volume of literature on the topic. It is almost impossible to summarize the writings in order to come to a few concrete conclusions. As one scholar has written, "the pace of events is so swift, the weaknesses of besieged state institutions so great, the rules governing the relationship between the state and its citizens so unclear, that every day in this unfolding revolution dawns as a new day."[45]

Analysts are, in some instances, in complete disagreement on the lessons of the Arab Spring. For instance, Marc Lynch, an associate professor of political science at George Washington University writes "This unified narrative of change, and the rise of a new, popular pan-Arabism directed against regimes, is perhaps the greatest revelation of the uprisings."[46] Geoffrey Aronson, a director at the Foundation for Middle East Peace, writes however, "It is a fairly safe bet that, notwithstanding the common themes of the

---

[44]Thomas Friedman, "Pray, Hope, Prepare," *New York Times*, April 12, 2011, http://www.nytimes.com/2011/04/13/opinion/13friedman.html (accessed January 2012).

[45]Geoffrey Aronson, "How the Arab Spring Presages a Shifting World Order," *Foreign Policy*, May 17, 2011, http://mideast.foreignpolicy.com/posts/2011/05/17/ how_the_arab_spring_presages_a_shifting_world_order (accessed January 2012).

[46]Marc Lynch, "The Big Think Behind the Arab Spring," *Foreign Policy*, November 28, 2011, http://www.foreignpolicy.com/articles/2011/11/28/the_big_think (accessed December 2011).

Arab Spring, Pan-Arabism is dead."[47] Further yet in *The Atlantic*, Massoud Hayoun

writes that a renewed pan-Arabism movement will likely cause the region to question

who truly is and is not Arab, which will have its own potentially destabilizing effect.[48]

While it is understandable that in the midst of an ongoing event like the Arab Spring

there would be conflicting ideas about the underlying themes, the unsettled nature of the

event creates challenges in applying its lessons to other parts of the world.

The Brookings Institute published an article on the one-year anniversary of the

Arab Spring that highlighted five lessons from the revolts. The five major lessons

outlined were (1) the impossible is possible, (2) the impossible, though, is still highly

unlikely, (3) Islamists are the future, (4) instability can be constructive, (5) caution is

overrated.[49] The article makes clear that the final lesson addresses the lack of

involvement by the Obama administration and criticizes the administration's perceived

slow response to the Arab Spring. Specifically, the article notes "Nor is it a time,

however, for excessive caution and slow deliberation. While the Obama administration

insists it has chosen the 'right side,' Arab activists, protestors, and revolutionaries seem

to disagree."[50] Internally at home, former U.S. presidential candidate Michelle Bachman

accused President Obama of abandoning America's enduring relationship with Egyptian

President Hosni Mubarak by supporting the protestors, which she claims has resulted in

---

[47] Aronson, "How the Arab Spring Presages a Shifting World Order."

[48] Massoud Hayoun, "Coming Arab Identity Crisis- Arab Spring Spurs Hopes For Regional Unity," *The Atlantic*, March 8, 2012.

[49] Brookings Institute Five Lessons from Arab revolts.

[50] Ibid.

the Muslim Brotherhood taking power in Egypt and thus, threatening Israel's security.[51]

Fouad Ajami, one of the most notable Middle Eastern analysts disagrees: "Hosni

Mubarak was the author of his own demise." Ajami believes that America should not be

assumed to be the cause of every event occurring around the world.[52]

Thomas Friedman predicted the competing agendas at the center of the Arab

Spring revolutions in his book *The Lexus and the Olive Tree*. In his book he describes the

convergence of two somewhat conflicting desires in places like the Middle East–the

desire for modern and free-market type ideals (the "Lexus") while at the same time

protecting the old cultural values and idiosyncrasies of tribal and religious societies (the

"Olive Tree"). "The new Lexus-like values of "democracy," "free elections," "citizen

rights" and "modernity" will have to compete with some very old Olive Tree ideas and

passions."[53] Assumedly, these ideas could apply to any revolution in North Korea–with

the understanding that the closed nature of the society to Western values might limit the

influence of the Lexus.

---

[51]Hunter Walker, "Michele Bachmann Blasts Obama for Not 'standing by' Israel and Mubarak," Politicker.com, February 9, 2012, http://politicker.com/2012/02/ 09/michele-bachmann-blasts-obama-for-not-standing-by-israel-and-mubarak/ (accessed May 20, 2012).

[52]Fouad Ajami, "Five Myths About the Arab Spring," *Washington Post*, January 12, 2011, http://www.washingtonpost.com/opinions/five-myths-about-the-arab-spring/ 2011/12/21/gIQA32TVuP_story.html(accessed May 20, 2012).

[53]Thomas Friedman, "In the Arab World, It's the Past Vs. The Future," *New York Times*, November 26, 2011, http://www.nytimes.com/2011/11/27/opinion/sunday/ Friedman-in-the-arab-world-its-the-past-vs-the-future.html?_r=2&ref=opinion (accessed April 28, 2012).

CHAPTER 3

RESEARCH METHODOLOGY

This research thesis seeks to analyze the conditions present in selected Arab Spring revolutions and apply those conditions to North Korea to determine the likelihood of whether a similar type of popular uprising could occur. To do so, a comparative analysis method will be utilized to assess selected criteria that were present during the Arab Spring then compare those criteria with the current conditions in North Korea. Of course, as stated in previous chapters, not all Arab Spring revolutions have happened in the same manner. However, this thesis seeks to identify common themes among those revolutions and apply those themes to the North Korean situation.

The pre-revolution governments of Egypt, Libya, and Syria shared characteristics common to the North Korean government and, accordingly, provide the best means for comparison. Choosing those countries does not dismiss the possibility that similar conditions existed in other revolutions that occurred in Tunisia, Yemen, Bahrain, or Jordan. Therefore, the researcher acknowledges that some elements in North Korea could be more closely related to the countries not chosen in this study. However, in an effort to provide a clear and focused analysis, the examination will be limited to Egypt, Libya, and Syria as compared to North Korea.

Multiple criteria could be used to conduct the comparison between the above mentioned Arab Spring revolutions and North Korea. In keeping with the effort to keep the research focused, though, three specific criteria, frequently cited in research materials as primary contributing reasons for the Arab Spring, were selected for analysis.

27

The first criterion is the geo-political situation of the surrounding countries, both regionally and globally. The geo-political environment was selected because vital interests of certain regional and global nations may cause their governments' to act, or in some cases not act, in the instance of unrest occurring in North Korea, which in turn could influence the success of that revolution.

The second criterion is the examined nation's security forces and their role in society. This criterion was selected because the strength of a nation's military and its loyalty to the government could determine the regime's ability to suppress a popular uprising.

The final criterion is the concept of the "network." This criterion was selected because the use of social networking tools like Twitter, Facebook, and Skype have been widely recognized as playing an integral role in rallying support for the uprisings in the Middle East, but is not limited to technologies such as cell phones and internet use. In addition to the impact of the social network, other networking options will be examined, such as organization of opposition groups, external active Diasporas and additional relevant factors that assist or hinder citizens from gathering and organizing.

As noted, the researcher has selected Egypt, Libya, and Syria because each country has shared characteristics with the North Korean government and possibly its society. In the case of Egypt, the nation's military enjoys a central role in society similar to the military's role in North Korea. Hosni Mubarak and former Egyptian Minister of Defense Abu Ghazala shared a vision that would expand the domestic role of the military to include economic initiatives.[54] The policies gave the Egyptian military a central role in domestic politics that has continued following the Arab Spring. Kim Jong II sought to insulate his power by buying the loyalty of the military when he introduced the policy of Songun, or "military first" in 1995. The policy puts the military as the top priority in North Korean society. Whether it occurred as a driver for economic change, in the case of Egypt, or to assure the loyalty of the military leadership, as in North Korea, the military's central role is a crucial factor in society.

Libya is a useful comparison because Moammar Gaddafi and Kim Jong II shared a similar cult-like following as unquestioned leaders of their respective countries. Prior to the Arab Spring, Gaddafi and Kim were central to the respective ideologies of Libya and North Korea. Gaddafi stated as late as February 2011, during an interview with Christine Amanpour, "They love me. All my people with me, they love me," and "They will die to protect me, my people."[55] The North Korean leadership has similarly used the early part of 2012 to build the cult-like persona of their new leader Kim Jong Un. Despite his youth, North Korean leaders have sought to build the persona and competence of Kim Jong Un. Some observers have noted he has been made to look like his revered grandfather Kim II Sung, "probably strategically."[56] As an example of the North Korean "play book" for

---

[54]LTC Stephan H. Gotowicki, *The Military in Egyptian Society* (Washington, DC: National Defense University, 1997), 110.

[55]Christian Amanpour, *Interview with Libyan President Moammar Gaddafi* (2011), Tripoli, Libya, http://abcnews.go.com/International/christiane-amanpour-interviews-libyas-moammar-gadhafi/story?id=13019942#.T5w6U6vsvD9 (accessed March 2011).

[56]Jean H. Lee and Sam Kim, "Kim Jong Un, North Korea New Leader, Fashions Himself as Reincarnation of Kim II Sung," *Huffington Post*, January 17, 2012,

building their leaders' images, North Korean state television reported in 1994 that Kim Jong Il had eleven "hole-in-ones" in his first attempt at golf. While this feat may seem ludicrous, this is how North Korea systematically constructs their leaders' super-natural persona.[57] Therefore, this thesis compares the demise of Gaddafi to the situation for the North Korean leadership.

Finally, Syria was selected for examination and comparison because Syrian President Bashar Al Assad assumed power under circumstances like those by which Kim Jong Il and now Kim Jong Un rose to power. Hafez Al Assad, Bashar Al Assad's father, seized power in Syria in a bloodless coup in November 1970. Hafez Al Assad ruled Syria for three decades and passed away in 2000. Following his father's death, Bashar Al-Assad was handed power in hereditary succession.[58] Likewise, following the death of Kim Il Sung and now Kim Jong Il, a transition to a familial successor has occurred. Additionally, Syria merits examination because of the support that it receives from Iran. The Shiite dominated theocracy provides support to the Syrian regime through training and financing. China performs a similar role for the North Korean regime.

This research thesis focuses on articles and writings that addressed the following: (1) links between the Arab Spring and North Korea; (2) reasons that ignited, perpetuated

---

http://www.huffingtonpost.com/2012/01/07/kim-jong-un_n_1191337.html (accessed May 20, 2012).

[57]Mind-Boggling "facts" About Kim Jong-Il, *Herald Sun*, December 19, 2011, http://www.heraldsun.com.au/news/more-news/from-fashion-icon-to-golf-pro-mind-boggling-facts-about-kim-jong-il/story-e6frf7lf-1226226100974 (accessed May 20, 2012).

[58]Robert M. Danin, "Remembering Hafez Al-Assad," Council on Foreign Relations: Middle East Matters, entry posted November 11, 2011, http://blogs.cfr.org/danin/2011/11/11/remembering-hafez-al-assad/ (accessed March 2011).

and defined the Middle Eastern uprisings; and (3) analysis performed following the death of Kim Jong II. The approach taken was to use various search engines to identify research that had been conducted from previously completed studies, major news outlet reporting, and scholarly opinions and analysis.

This topic required mostly qualitative research to determine the key factors that ignited, perpetuated, and defined the Arab Spring revolutions as compared to the situation in North Korea. Therefore, all conclusions are written in descriptive expressions. Certain quantitative measurements such as size of an army or number of internet users are included herein but the majority of information is qualitative in nature.

CHAPTER 4

ANALYSIS

Geo-political Environment–"The Neighborhood"

Egypt

The U.S. government has experienced a complicated relationship with Egypt

since Anwar Sadat took power in 1970–a relationship similar to the American

relationship with Saudi Arabia. In both relationships, the U.S. has foregone its role as the

world's preeminent democracy-sponsoring state and supported oppressive dictatorships

because of the vital natural resources present in Egypt and Saudi Arabia and the pro-

American views of their leaders. Prior to the Arab Spring, the U.S. provided Egypt with

approximately $1.3 billion annually in military and economic aid, in large part because of

Hosni Mubarak's pro-U.S. stance, Egypt's unlimited access to the Suez Canal and its lack

of provocation towards Israel.[59] With tacit American approval therefore, Mubarak ruled

Egypt with impunity, clinging to power by oppressing potential political opposition and

ignoring brutal police tactics against Egyptian citizens.

While supporting the autocratic Mubarak regime, the U.S. government also

funded non-governmental organizations that focused on democratic reforms in certain

Arab states, funding that, according to a recent *New York Times* article, played a role in

---

[59]Jill Doughtery and Chris Lawrence, "Egypt Warned U.S. Aid at Risk," *CNN*, February 3, 2012, http://security.blogs.cnn.com/2012/02/03/egypt-warned-u-s-aid-at-risk/?hpt=hp_t3 (accessed March 2012).

fomenting the Arab Spring.[60] This splintered approach to the Middle East created a big

problem for the Obama administration when reacting to the events in the Arab Spring. It

was in America's interest to champion, as President Obama stated in his Cairo speech,

real democracy, but, in so doing, the administration risked losing the support of a key

Middle Eastern ally. Ultimately, the U.S. supported the Mubarak's administration

resignation and democratic elections, which subsequently produced huge gains for the

Muslim Brotherhood, a known Islamist organization that opposed Mubarak's pro-U.S.

views.

The sudden nature of the Egyptian revolt forced the U.S. to choose between

supporting democratic reforms that it has historically preached and supporting an

historical ally who, although dictatorial and oppressive, provided stability to the region.

The rise of the Muslim Brotherhood underscores the riskiness of the path the U.S. chose

to follow, as America now faces the potential of an unfriendly regime and a possibly

unstable Egypt, a risk that Israeli journalist Zvi Bar'el stated was inherent in supporting

democracy. Bar'el wrote "it's impossible to want democracy and also oppose the Muslim

Brotherhood, to want Mubarak's swift departure and also insure that the next presidential

candidate won't be from the left."[61]

Although the situation in Egypt carries risk for America, the Obama

administration nonetheless believes that America can still impact a transition to a stable

---

[60]Ron Nixon, "U.S. Groups Helped Nurture Arab Uprisings," *New York Times*, April 14, 2011, http://www.nytimes.com/2011/04/15/world/15aid.html?_r=1&hp (accessed April 2012).

[61]Zvi Bar'el, "What Exactly Does the U.S. Want from Egypt," *Hareetz*, February 8, 2011, http://www.haaretz.com/print-edition/news/what-exactly-does-the-u-s-want-from-egypt-1.341903 (accessed April 2012).

democracy. As Secretary Clinton said, "These revolutions are not ours—they are not by us, for us, or against us. But we do have a role. We have the resources, capabilities and expertise to support those who seek peaceful, meaningful democratic reform."[62]

The U.S. is not the only globally focused nation that finds itself placed in a tough position by events in the Middle East. As Dr. Robert Freedman of the Strategic Studies Institute of the U.S. Army War College noted, "The Arab Spring caught Russia, as it did the United States and indeed the countries affected, by surprise."[63] Initially, Russia was unsure of how to proceed with regards to the demonstrations in Egypt. Russian interests in Egypt were far smaller than their interests in Libya and Syria because the pro-U.S. Mubarak regime had limited Russian involvement. The Egyptian revolution then, affords Russia both the removal of a staunch American ally and an opportunity to paint the U.S. as meddling in other countries' affairs. Freedman notes that "President Dmitry Medvedev and other Kremlin leaders took a tough line in response, and—in an almost Cold War-era reaction—asserted that the revolts in the Arab world were instigated by 'outside forces' that were also trying to topple the Russian government."[64]

Although the Egyptian revolution creates an opportunity for Russia, the rise of the Muslim Brotherhood to an elevated power status in Egypt also creates concerns. Russia is

---

[62]Josh Rogin, "Clinton Confronts the Paradox of America's Role in the Arab Spring," *Foreign Policy*, November 7, 2011, http://thecable.foreignpolicy.com/posts/2011/11/07/clinton_confronts_the_paradox_of_america_s_role_in_the_arab_spring (accessed March 2012).

[63]Robert O. Freedman, "The Arab Spring's Challenge to Moscow," *The Journal of International Security Affairs* 21 (Fall/Winter 2011), http://www.securityaffairs.org/issues/2011/21/freedman.php (accessed March 2012).

[64]Ibid.

dealing with independence-seeking Islamist groups in the North Caucasus region, and fears that the rise of Islamist political organizations in the Middle East could inspire similar uprisings in Russia. Vladimir Putin accused the West of inciting democracy-seeking revolutions that could have negative effects for other parts of the world, "such as Russia's North Caucasus."[65] Nonetheless, Russian intervention in Egypt has been minimal, with Russia electing to exert more influence during protests in Libya and Syria, two states with much closer ties to Moscow.

For Saudis, the fall of the Mubarak regime creates its own host of problems. Saudi Arabia is arguably the most powerful regional player in the Middle East. It is a Sunni-dominated society ruled by the House of Saud, an autocratic regime with similarities to those in Libya, Syria, and Egypt. Saudi Arabia practices the most conservative form of Islam, known as Salafism, which bars opposition to rulers, limiting opposition groups and liberal thought.[66] The Saudi regime does, however, provide religious counter-balance to the rising influence of Shiite-dominated Iran in the region. In October 2011, the monarchy experienced small protests by Shiites in eastern cities in Saudi Arabia, which Saudi leaders blamed on Iranian agents. Saudi leaders claimed Iran had been trying to ignite a revolt similar to the Arab Spring revolutions in the Sunni rival nation.

With a Shiite neighbor eager to foment revolution in Sunni nations, Saudi Arabia was quick to intervene in Bahrain, a fellow Sunni nation facing its own protests. Rachel

---

[65]Serge Korepin and Shalini Sharan, *What Does the Arab Spring Mean For Russia, Central Asia and the Caucasus?* (Washington, DC: Center for Strategic and International Studies, September 2011), 8-9.

[66]Obaid, "There Will Be No Uprising in Saudi Arabia."

Bronson of the Foreign Policy Research Institute wrote that Saudi Arabia's deployment of troops to Bahrain was a rational response. Bahrain is economically and geo-politically critical to Saudi Arabia because of its proximity and also its demographics. Bahrain is Sunni-led; however it has a Shi'a population of approximately 70 percent. Directly across the shared border in Saudi Arabia sits a Shi'a population of 15 percent in the Saudi eastern provinces. The large public protests in Bahrain could have inspired similar demonstrations. Saudi Arabia was quick to act to ensure that discontent did not spread against its government. Bronson writes, "Any unrest there has the potential to spill over into the Kingdom and upend global oil markets."[67]

The Saudis refrained from intervening in Egypt, however, because the rise of the Muslim Brotherhood, which also practices Salafism, appears to be a positive development for the Saudis. During Mubarak's rule, Muslim Brotherhood members took refuge in Saudi Arabia.[68] To date, Riyadh appears willing to involve itself in certain Arab Spring revolutions to protect its power base, but does not act when it believes the outcome would benefit the Kingdom's national interests.

Of all the players in the region, Israel may have the most to lose in the tide of revolution coming to the Middle East. For decades, Israel enjoyed relative peace with Egypt to its south, secure in the knowledge that the Mubarak regime garnered support from the U.S. because of its peaceful co-existence with the Jewish state. In some cases,

---

[67]Rachel Bronson, *Saudi Arabia's Intervention in Bahrain* (Philadelphia, PA: Foreign Policy Research Institute, 2011).

[68]John R. Bradley, "Saudi Arabia's Invisible Hand in the Arab Spring," *Foreign Affairs*, October 13, 2011, http://www.foreignaffairs.com/articles/136473/john-r-bradley/saudi-arabias-invisible-hand-in-the-arab-spring (accessed March 2012).

Mubarak even limited Palestinian movement into Egypt, further bolstering Israel's position in the region.

Some Middle Eastern scholars speculate that Arab unity may finally be possible. Egyptian writer Hassan Hanafi, noted that because of the uprisings, "Arab unity —long a distant ideal in a region better known for its fragmentation and ideological bickering—is an objective reality."[69] The growth of this Arab Nationalism could increase animosity towards Israel. Prior to the Arab Spring revolutions, Israel enjoyed a somewhat peaceful co-existence with Egypt, Jordan, and other Arab nations. While Israel cannot be content surveying the new geo-political realities of the region, it cannot do much to reverse recent events. Daniel Byman, Director of the Saban Center for Middle East policy, believes the revolutions could strain U.S.-Israel relations because the U.S. must appear to support democratic movements, regardless of their impact on Israel's security.[70]

Libya

For the U.S., circumstances in Libya differ from those in Egypt. The conditions that made the Egyptian revolution problematic for America (i.e., the pro-U.S. leaders versus the need to publicly support democracy), were absent in Libya. Unlike Mubarak, Moammar Gaddafi has long been an enemy to the U.S.. Still, the Obama administration was reluctant to become militarily involved.

The Libyan Arab Spring grew more violent than the uprisings in Egypt and Tunisia. In February 2012, Wolfram Lacher, a business risk analyst specializing in North

---

[69]Lynch, "The Big Think Behind the Arab Spring."

[70]Daniel Bynam, "Israel's Pessimistic View of the Arab Spring," *Washington Quarterly* 34, no. 3 (2011): 123-36.

Africa, wrote that the revolts in Libya escalated because of the Gaddafi regime's violent response to the protests. The widespread killing of civilians by the Libyan security apparatus forced tribes, rebels, and even Libyan Army units to oppose Gaddhafi.[71] Likewise, the growing humanitarian crisis made it easier for the U.S. to commit military forces to support the rebel organizations. President Obama's stated reason for military involvement was that Gaddafi's "forces started going city to city, town by town to brutalize men, women and children."[72] Pressure from European nations however, namely Great Britain and France, was even more crucial in gaining U.S. support.

British Prime Minister David Cameron and French President Nicolas Sarkozy led the international calls for intervention into Libya. According to Lance Elliot who wrote in *Time*, Britain and France wanted to act for two reasons. First, the U.S. took the lead in the Global War on Terror and was deeply involved in Afghanistan and, until recently, Iraq. Britain, France, and the larger NATO alliance could not simply rely on the U.S. to take the lead in every international crisis and appeared to recognize that the European powers likewise have a role to ensure global stability. Secondly, Elliot argues that Britain and France came to the conclusion that there would be consequences for failing to act to stop

[71]Wolfram Lacher, "The Libyan Revolution: Old Elites and New Political Forces," *German Institute for International and Security Affairs* 27 (February 2012): 11-14, http://www.swp.berlin.org/fileadmin/contents/products/research_papers/2012_RP06_ass.pdf#page=11 (accessed April 2012).

[72]Mark Landler, "For Obama, Some Vindication of Approach to War," *New York Times*, October 20, 2011, http://www.nytimes.com/2011/10/21/world/africa/qaddafis-death-is-latest-victory-for-new-us-approach-to-war.html (accessed April 2012).

the growing humanitarian crisis.[73] The European nations were much more likely to feel the effects of a Libyan humanitarian crisis, which likely would have resulted in a large number of refugees attempting to flee into Europe.

For Russia, the Libyan crisis created its own set of challenges to navigate. Robert O. Freedman, in an article "The Arab Spring's Challenge to Moscow," described Russia's stance on Libya as indecisive, terming it the "zigzag policy."[74] Initially, Russia opposed both sanctions and the no-fly zone, but ultimately allowed them by abstaining (along with China) from voting on United Nations (UN) Resolution 1973, which permitted NATO intervention.[75] Freedman attributes Russian indecisiveness in part to disagreements between President Dmitry Medvedev and Prime Minister Vladimir Putin about how to proceed.[76] Additionally, Freedman states that Russia was unwilling to oppose Arab consensus regarding the need for Western intervention in light of the League of Arab States' plea to the West.[77] Russia did not want to jeopardize its involvement in the Middle East by opposing the majority of Arab states and therefore Russia was forced to support the Arab movements while trying to minimize any strengthening of the U.S. in the Middle East. Kori Schake, a research fellow at the Hoover Institute, believes that Russia and China may have had second thoughts about

---

[73]Michael Elliott, "Viewpoint: How Libya Became a French and British War Read More," *Time*, March 19, 2011, http://www.time.com/time/world/article/ 0,8599,2060412,00.html (accessed March 2012).

[74]Freedman, "The Arab Spring's Challenge to Moscow."

[75]U.S. United Nations, Security Council, Resolution 1973, UN Resolution 1973 (New York, NY, 2011), 3.

[76]Freedman, "The Arab Spring's Challenge to Moscow."

[77]Ibid.

clearing Western intervention because it gave NATO and the U.S. a mandate to act in cases such as Libya.[78] As discussed in detail, below, the situation in Syria suggests that both China and Russia are unwilling to grant the Western powers that mandate again.

Syria

Unlike the cases of Egypt and Libya, the uprisings in Syria have presented a more difficult set of circumstances for the international community in choosing how to respond. Syria differs largely because many more nations have vested interests in the outcome of its revolution. Because of its location and it's alliance with the region's Shiite-led regimes, the consequences of Al-Assad's fall could have an incredibly large effect in the region. Thomas Friedman acknowledged that the Tunisian, Egyptian, Libyan, and Yemeni revolutions resulted in implosions of their governments, but he believes that a change in Syrian leadership will cause an explosion, because Syria provides direct support to Lebanon and Hezbollah. That relationship affects the security of Israel, especially in the Golan Heights, home to the border between Syria and Israel. Moreover, because Lebanon and Syria are proxy states for Iran, the Syrian version of the Arab Spring is the first that directly threatens Iran's national interests. Iran relies heavily on support from the Al-Assad regime and continues to funnel weapons to Hezbollah through Syria. Iraq, on the other hand, is a fragile democracy in need of a secure border that will block the flow of jihadists from Syria.[79]

---

[78]Kori Schake, "Lessons of the Libya War," *Defining Ideas*, October 13, 2011, http://www.hoover.org/publications/defining-ideas/article/96531 (accessed April 2012).

[79]Thomas Friedman, "If Syria Blows Up," *Pittsburgh Post Gazette*, http://www.post-gazette.com/stories/opinion/perspectives/thomas-l-friedman-if-syria-blows-up-299069/ (accessed April 2012).

Furthermore, opposition groups in Syria are not as well-armed or well-organized as those in Libya, and Syrian President Bashar Al Assad has refused to step down. Syria is ruled by the minority Alawite sect, a form of Islam similar to Shiites, while the majority of Syrians are Sunni Muslims. Alawites and Shiites differ on the deification of Ali, a direct descendent of the prophet Muhammad.[80] A minor difference that does not largely affect the Alawite-Shiite relationship. If Al-Assad were removed from power, the ensuing civil war could force every nation in the Middle East to choose sides, likely along Sunni-Shiite divides. Indeed, some nations are starting to take action on both sides. Reports suggest that Iranian Quds Force Commander Kassam Salimani is in Syria assisting with managing the war against opposition groups.[81] Saudi Arabian Foreign Minister Prince Saud al-Faisal called arming the FSA "an excellent idea."[82] Both sides appear to be preparing for a long conflict.

China and Russia have invested heavily in Syria and depend on the Assad regime's support. According to Ruslan Pukhov, head of the independent Center for Analysis of Strategies and Technologies, "He [Assad] is Russia's last remaining ally in

---

[80]Martin Kramer, "Syria's Alawis and Shi'ism," Geocities.com, http://www.geocities.com/martinkramerorg/Alawis.htm (accessed May 31, 2012).

[81]Zvi Bar'el, "Report: Top Iran Military Official Aiding Assad's Crackdown on Syria Opposition," *Hareetz*, February 6, 2012, http://www.haaretz.com/news/middle-east/report-top-iran-military-official-aiding-assad-s-crackdown-on-syria-opposition-1.411402 (accessed March 2012).

[82]Tony Karron, "Can Syria's Assad Fight His Way to Political Survival?" *Time.com*, February 28, 2012, http://globalspin.blogs.time.com/2012/02/28/syria-can-assad-fight-his-way-to-political-survival/ (accessed April 2012).

the Middle East, allowing it to preserve influence in the region."[83] The Russian-Syrian

relationship dates back to the Cold War era when the Soviet Union supported the coup

conducted by Assad's father, Hafez Al-Assad. Analysts estimate that Russian military

arms deals with Syria exceed $4 billion.[84] Additionally, the Syrian port city of Tartus is

home to a leased Russian naval base. Russia also recently moved military resources and

Russian Marines into the region in response to the lengthy revolt.[85]

As the uprising continues, the U.S. and European Union will increasingly find

themselves at odds with Russia and China over Syria. China and Russia have both

blocked efforts by the U.S. and European nations to pass a UN Security Council

Resolution to force sanctions on Syria in an effort to stop the killing of innocent Syrians

and the removal of Al-Assad from power. Fouad Ajami, a senior fellow at Stanford

University's Hoover Institute, has described the opposing geo-political external players

as the "Friends of Syria," mainly the U.S., European nations, and many Arab

governments versus the "Friends of the Syrian Regime," who are Russia, Iran, Hezbollah,

and China.[86]

---

[83]Vladimir Isachenko, "Russia Backs Assad, Last Friend in Arab World," *Associated Press*, January 29, 2012, http://news.yahoo.com/russia-backs-assad-last-friend-arab-world-101528682.html (accessed April 2012).

[84]Holly Yan, "Why China, Russia Won't Condemn Syrian Regime," *CNN*, February 5, 2012, http://articles.cnn.com/2012-02-05/middleeast/world_meast_syria-china-russia-relations_1_syrian-president-bashar-al-assad-syrian-government-syrian-regime?_s=PM:MIDDLEEAST (accessed April 2012).

[85]Ibid.

[86]Fouad Ajami, "America's Alibis For Not Helping Syria," *Hoover Daily Report*, February 24, 2012, http://www.hoover.org/news/daily-report/109346 (accessed April 2012).

More so than Egypt and Libya, Syria provides the closest model to the challenges that the various geo-political participants would face, if a similar situation occurred in North Korea. As discussed, the situation in Egypt was likely to stabilize due to the direct involvement of the nation's military leaders and the pressure that the U.S. could inflict through the threat of withholding economic aid. Likewise, Libya caused minimal geo-political tension because the stakes for China and Russia were not significant, so they abstained from challenging NATO intervention. Syria, on the other hand, is directly within Russia's sphere of influence and all of the world's global powers have a stake in the outcome. Likewise, in North Korea, each of the members of the six-party talks is likely to view a sudden collapse or revolution as greatly destabilizing to the entire region, with China and Russia having a substantial interest in maintaining the status quo and the U.S. would be interested in regime change.

North Korea

Any study of North Korea's geo-political situation needs to be discussed within the framework of nations that form the "six-party talks." The U.S., China, Russia, Japan, and South Korea join North Korea as the framework for the geo-political environment that exists in Northeast Asia. The six-party talks first took place in Beijing in August 2003.

China

In May 2011, Chinese President Hu Jintao spoke at a banquet in Beijing honoring the General Secretary of the Korean Workers' Party Kim Jong II, during which he said, "We will work hard to accelerate socialist construction in the two countries, promote interests common to the two sides and defend and promote the peace, stability and prosperity of the region."[87] The People's Republic of China is North Korea's largest supporter and ally because of their shared socialist governance styles, historical ties dating back to the Korean War, and a relationship of need for both nations. However, China's foreign policy towards North Korea and its larger policy towards Northeast Asia are more complicated. Official Chinese policy supports Korean unification if it is achieved in a peaceful manner and is generated through the Korean people themselves on both sides of the border.[88] However, it is hard to imagine how a popular uprising, similar to the Arab Spring, could be executed in North Korea in a peaceful way.

Gordon Flake, Executive Director of the Mansfield Foundation, spoke to The Korea Society in May 2011 in New York City outlining China's view of its relationship to North Korea. Flake described the relationship being much more communist party to communist party than state to state.[89] As China's strength grows in all elements of national power (diplomacy, information, military, and economics), the task of forming one unified foreign policy towards North Korea is becoming increasingly harder. In other words, different institutions in the Chinese government are arriving at diverging views of

---

[87]Denny Roy, Ph.D., "China and the Korean Peninsula: Beijing's Pyongyang Problem and Hope," *Asia-Pacific Security Studies* 3, no. 1 (January 2004): 1-4, http://www.apcss.org/Publications/APSSS/ChinaandtheKoreanPeninsula.pdf (accessed April 2012).

[88]Gill Bates, *China's North Korea Policy: Assessing Interests and Influences* (Washington, DC: United States Institute for Peace, July 2011), 1-16.

[89]Gordon Flake, "China's Approach to North Korea" The Korea Society, May 5, 2011, http://www.koreasociety.org/ policy/policy/ chinas_approach_to_north_korea.html (accessed April 2012).

what the relationship should be with North Korea.[90] However, there are a few common themes that can be determined based on China's national interests.

First, the Chinese government has and will likely continue to support the North Korean regime because of the balance of power that the regime brings to the Korean peninsula and Northeast Asia. With the pro-American government in South Korea growing ever stronger, China needs to support North Korea with valuable resources to maintain that security buffer for the Chinese. China has regarded U.S. foreign policy in Asia as a containment strategy to limit Chinese influence. It includes the strengthening of alliances with Japan, South Korea, and Taiwan, as well as increasing military cooperation on projects such as missile defense and naval exercises.[91] Secondly, a sudden collapse of the North Korean regime will lead to a large refugee problem that will affect China significantly because of its 880-mile shared border with North Korea. Thirdly, Chinese foreign policy decisions are mostly formed by what is best economically for the People's Republic of China. China's investment and trade with South Korea is at an all-time high, 70 times greater than its economic cooperation with North Korea. China would not take any action or policy position that would risk its economic prosperity at risk.

A notion exists amongst China watchers that Beijing's foreign policy development is becoming increasingly more difficult. Chinese institutions, such as the Chinese Communist Party, the People's Liberation Army, and the economic policy

---

[90]Bates, *China's North Korea Policy,* 1-16.

[91]Hakkeun Jin, "A Study of China's Possible Military Intervention in the Event of Sudden Change in North Korea" (Master's thesis, Command and General Staff College, Fort Leavenworth, KS, 2011), 13, http://cgsc.contentdm.oclc.org/cdm/singleitem/ collection/p4013coll2/id/2784/rec/1 (accessed March 2012).

makers, have grown stronger and more nuanced in their views of how to deal with North

Korea. Noted China analyst Jonathan Pollack outlines three differing views inside the

Chinese government institutions as they relate to North Korea. They are: (1) a "hard line"

approach, which believes some Chinese leaders are weary of North Korea's pursuit of

nuclear weapons because with it brings increased U.S. military and diplomatic efforts to

the region, (2) a "stability-first" approach, which strongly supports the status quo and,

thus the maintenance of North Korea's security buffer along the Chinese border, and (3)

an economic approach that only seeks to increase economic cooperation with North

Korea. Pollack believes there are Chinese leaders who disagree on the best approach, but

all agree the "stability first" approach is the most straightforward.[92] China's overarching

desire is regional stability. Jae Woo Choo, assistant professor of Chinese foreign policy at

Kyung Hee University in South Korea argues, "After all, it [China's goal] is not about

securing influence over North Korean affairs but is about peaceful management of the

relationship with the intent to preserve the status quo of the peninsula."[93] Therefore, one

conclusion could be that China's policies in the event of a popular uprising in North

Korea would be to maintain the status quo by supporting the Kim regime to stabilize the

situation. Chinese response could come in the form of economic aid to the North Korean

people or diplomatic efforts similar to its actions to limit U.S. intervention efforts in

Syria.

---

[92]Bona Kim, "China's Policy Towards North Korea Redefined," *Daily North Korea*, http://www.dailynk.com/english/read.php?cataId=nk00100&num=5550 (accessed May 2012).

[93]Jayshree Bajoria, "The China-North Korea Relationship," *Council on Foreign Relations*, October 7, 2010, http://www.cfr.org/china/china-north-korea-relationship/p11097 (accessed April 2012).

South Korea

South Korean policy towards North Korea has been somewhat uneven over the

last 15 years. In 1998, Korean President Kim Dae Jung implemented the "Sunshine

Policy" towards North Korea that outlined a framework for interdependence between the

two nations and decreased hostility on the Korean peninsula. The policy addressed four

major points: (1) no absorption of North Korea in the process of unification,

(2) intolerance of any armed provocation destructive to peace, (3) the principle of

reciprocity, and (4) separation of the economy from politics.[94] President Roh Moo Hyun,

elected in 2003, continued the policy. At this point, U.S. and South Korean relations were

on the decline due to conflicting policies between the liberal Roh administration and the

conservative Bush administration on how to best address North Korea's pursuit of

nuclear weapons. President Roh wanted to maintain a non-hostile approach to North

Korea, while the Bush administration desired a hard line approach.[95] In 2008, South

Korea elected conservative candidate President Lee Myung-bak. With his election came

the end of the Sunshine Policy and a different tone in relations with North Korea.

Recent North Korean actions have exacerbated the tension between Seoul and

Pyongyang. In March 2010, a South Korean naval vessel, the Cheonan, sunk off the coast

of the Korean peninsula killing 46 sailors. The ensuing South Korean investigation

concluded the vessel sunk because of an external explosion, implicating a North Korean

[94]Kyung-suk Chae, "The Future of the Sunshine Policy: Strategies for Survival," *East-Asian Review* 14, no. 4 (Winter 2002): 2-6, http://www.ieas.or.kr/vol14_4/ 14_4_1.pdf (accessed April 2012).

[95]Katharine Moon, "South Korean-U.S. Relations," *Asian Perspective* 28, no. 4 (2004): 42-43, http://www.asianperspective.org/articles/v28n4-c.pdf (accessed April 2012).

torpedo or mine. In November 2010, North Korea shelled into Yeongpyong Island off the western coast of South Korea that killing multiple South Korean soldiers and civilians. These incidents continue to deteriorate the relationship between North and South Korea. While there may have been signs of a thawing of hostilities in the late 1990s and early 2000s, those signs have disappeared.

For much of the post-Korean war history, South Korea has had a long-term policy of anticipated unification at some point. That idea persists, as successive administrations have maintained a Unification Ministry. Unification Minister Yu Woo Ik has stated that unification remains a long-term goal and preparation is underway in the event it does occur, but that South Korea is in no way hoping for regime collapse in North Korea.[96] This caution suggests that South Korea will not take any action to promote instability in North Korea.

United States

Since 2008, when both Presidents Lee and Obama were elected, the U.S.-Republic of Korea alliance has rebounded. The Congressional Research Service reported in 2011 that U.S. and South Korean relations "were arguably at their best state in decades." The report outlines the Obama administration's policy towards the situation on the Korean peninsula as a joint approach with South Korea of "strategic patience." The joint approach insists future negotiations with North Korea must include the six-party

---

[96]South Korea's Unification Plan, *Spiegel*, March 10, 2012, http://www.spiegel. de/international/world/0,1518,820577,00.html (accessed April 2012).

nations and that North Korea must be willing to take "irreversible steps" to denuclearizing.[97]

The North Korean nuclear weapons issue and the growing strength of China remain the two largest issues confronting U.S. involvement in Northeast Asia. The current U.S. administration is strengthening and maintaining its alliances with South Korea and Japan. The strengthening of these alliances offsets China's growing power in the region and provides a united front against a nuclear North Korea. The U.S. will probably continue to emphasize the diplomatic element of national power to influence China's relationship with North Korea, while maintaining the military alliances with Seoul and Tokyo.

Regime collapse in Pyongyang is not in the best interest of the U.S. In Egypt and Libya, the U.S. was able to support regime change for a couple reasons. First, military involvement in Libya was not going to force Russia, China, or any other nation from intervening on behalf of Gaddafi. The fact that China and Russia chose not to veto the UN Security Council Resolution paved the way for U.S. and NATO intervention. Secondly, the relationship between senior Egyptian and U.S. military leaders ensured that a regime change in Egypt would not result in chaos throughout the country that could de-stabilize the entire region. A similar assumption is impossible in North Korea, as the U.S. has no relationship with North Korean military leaders. China has vital national interests at stake to oppose regime change in North Korea, plus there is no stabilizing institution in North Korea that would be able to oversee a transition. It is nearly impossible to predict

---

[97]Mark E. Manyin, *U.S.-South Korea Relations* (Washington, DC: Congressional Research Service, November 28, 2011), 2, http://www.fas.org/sgp/crs/row/R41481.pdf (accessed April 2012).

what actions would be taken by North Korean military leaders. Chinese and People's Liberation Army leaders might convince the North Korean military to maintain peace, but the resources probably do not exist to meet all the needs of the population. Therefore, it is in the best interest of the U.S. that stability remains on the Korean peninsula. The U.S. can strengthen its military alliances with South Korea and Japan while working towards a peaceful negotiation with North Korea on their nuclear weapons program.

Russia

Since the fall of the Soviet Union in 1991, Russia's influence over North Korea and its involvement in larger regional issues has diminished greatly. Prior to the Soviet break-up, North Korea relied heavily on Moscow's military and economic support to maintain the Cold War balance of power that existed on the Korean Peninsula. However, Moscow's influence waned in the 1990s and 2000s. Russian Prime Minister Vladimir Putin attempted to strengthen ties to North Korea by visiting Pyongyang in July 2002. According to Sung Chull Kim, who wrote *Engagement with North Korea, A Viable Alternative,* Putin's goal was to open some economic trade with North Korea. Kim Jong II welcomed these initiatives because he felt he could use the Russian offer as leverage to persuade China to increase its economic aid to North Korea.

Russia was added to the six-party talks that first took place in Beijing in August 2003. Both North Korea and China requested Russia be included because both nations felt Russian involvement would balance the negotiations.[98] Russia has less invested in North Korea than China does, and Russia would favor a nuclear-free Korean peninsula

---

[98]Sung Chull Kim and David Chan-oong Kang, *Engagement with North Korea: A Viable Alternative* (Albany, NY: SUNY Press, 2009), 107.

because it provides security in the region. The current separation of the Koreas is in the best interest of Russia because it balances power in the region, which limits both China and the U.S. from being able to exert total influence.

Japan

Bruce Cumings, a distinguished Korean War scholar, argues that at its heart, North Korea is mainly an anti-Japanese endeavor. He observes that most of its ideology and history has been tied to anti-Japanese resistance predating the Korean War.[99] North Korea and Japan have a long history of conflict, which includes Japan's colonization of the Korean peninsula and more recent kidnappings of Japanese citizens conducted by North Korean agents. Japan plays a role similar to Russia's in the six-party talks. Because of Japan's geographic position in Northeast Asia, the U.S. and South Korea believe it should be included in negotiations to disarm North Korea.

Hideshi Takesada, a professor at the National Institute for Defense Studies in Tokyo has concluded that Japan's security is directly tied to the stability on the Korean peninsula. In his view, the Japanese feel most threatened by North Korea's nuclear weapons, but he also sees growing Chinese influence over the peninsula as a major concern.[100] If Takesada is right, Japan should pursue three goals that all result from the status quo on the Korean peninsula. First, Japan should assist South Korea and the U.S. in convincing North Korea to relinquish its nuclear weapons for overall regional stability.

---

[99]Bruce Cumings, *The Korean War: A History* (New York: Random House, Inc., 2010), 43.

[100]Hideshi Takesada, "The Birth of a Unified Korea," *The Brown Journal of World Affairs* 7, no. 1 (Winter/Spring 2001): 95, http://www.watsoninstitute.org/ bjwa/archive/8.1/Korea/Takesada.pdf (accessed April 2012).

Second, it should maintain its alliance with the U.S., both economically and militarily, to strengthen its position. Finally, the Japanese should work to improve relations with South Korea in an effort to balance the increasing South Korean-Chinese relations. Historically, Japan and South Korea have not enjoyed the greatest of relations, but must form a workable solution to stem the growth of Chinese power in Northeast Asia.

All parties involved seek to maintain stability in Northeast Asia. South Korea and the U.S. would favor a unified and democratic Korea, but several obstacles block that goal. First, Russia and more importantly China would oppose a unified Korean republic on their borders. China would lose its buffer zone and, assuming the U.S.-Republic of Korea relations remain strong, increased U.S. influence in East Asia. Secondly, it would be extremely hard for any nation to take military or diplomatic efforts to undermine the situation in North Korea without upsetting the balance. If collapse became imminent, Russia and China would veto any effort by the UN to intervene. Therefore, all parties involved will use their "soft" power (diplomacy, information, economic) to maintain the current situation and the current stability.

Role of the Military (Security Forces) in Society

Egypt

The Egyptian military is the most influential institution in Egyptian domestic society. The Egyptian military numbers approximately 470,000 soldiers in four service branches: army, navy, air force, and air defenses. It includes both career and conscript soldiers. Egypt's citizens generally have high regard for the military and believe it has their best interests in mind. These forces are led by the Minister of Defense while an additional 325,000 para-military forces in the Central Security Services are led by the

Minister of the Interior. These para-military forces are largely responsible for the violent crackdown on the civil liberties of Egyptian citizens.[101] Following Mubarak's ouster, the Egyptian military has taken responsibility during the transitional period, led by Mohamed Hussein Tantawi, head of Egypt's Supreme Council of Armed Forces. While the military has firmly taken control, the Central Security Services, as well as the Intelligence Services, present possible power struggles in the future. Only time will tell how the newly democratically elected leaders reconcile the powers of the different institutions.

The Egyptian military enjoys an elevated status in its society and has played a critical role in Egyptian politics since the overthrow of the monarchy in 1952. Hosni Mubarak commanded Egypt's Air Force prior to becoming the head of state, and his predecessor, Anwar Sadat, was also a career military officer. Retired Egyptian officers are involved in economic ventures such as hotels and other commercial initiatives that offer lucrative sources of income. Moreover, the military's budget is not subject to parliamentary approval.[102] Robert Springborg, a professor at the Naval Postgraduate School, described the Egyptian military as "a business conglomerate, like General Electric."[103]

---

[101] Anthony H. Cordesman, "If Mubarak Leaves: The Role of the Egyptian Military," Center for Strategic and International Studies, February 10, 2011, http://csis.org/publication/if-mubarak-leaves-role-us-military (accessed March 2012).

[102] Jacob G. Hornberger, "Egypt's Military Problem," Hornberger's Blog, entry posted July 18, 2011, http://www.fff.org/blog/jghblog2011-07-18.asp (accessed March 2012).

[103] Andrew S. Ross, "Egypt's Military, an Economic Giant, Now in Charge," *San Francisco Chronicle*, February 13, 2011, http://www.sfgate.com/cgi-bin/article.cgi?f=/c/a/2011/02/12/BU1V1HLVP6.DTL (accessed March 2012).

Peter Grier, a writer for the *Christian Science Monitor*, believes that the Egyptian military is the only institution in the country that could have pressured Mubarak to step down.[104] In *Time*, Tony Karon wrote that the Egyptian military recognized the "legitimacy" of the revolution and would not use force against protesters.[105] If these observers are right, one can conclude that the Egyptian military sided with demonstrators in order to maintain stability mindful that, in post-Mubarak Egypt, it would be the lone power broker in Egyptian society. In short, western journalists believe the Egyptian protesters forced out Mubarak's regime largely because senior Egyptian military leaders allowed them to do so.

Some Egyptians worry that the Supreme Council of Armed Forces and their leaders may be trying to increase its role in civil society in the post-Mubarak era. The military leadership has announced that it will push for a "declaration of basic principles" in the forming of a new Egyptian constitution, which the military is overseeing. *New York Times* Cairo bureau chief David Kirkpatrick has reported that the military leaders are trying to increase their role in society while protecting their economic ventures and defense budgets.[106] The Egyptian military's role in society is the closest model to the North Korean system of military control. Although the reaction of North Korea's military

---

[104]Peter Grier, "Mubarak Stepping Down in Egypt: Was It a Coup?" *Christian Science Monitor*, February 11, 2011, http://www.sfgate.com/cgi-bin/article.cgi?f=/c/a/2011/02/12/BU1V1HLVP6.DTL (accessed March 2012).

[105]Tony Karon, "Egyptian Military Proving to Be Rival Power Center to Mubarak," *Time*, February 2011, http://www.time.com/time/specials/packages/article/0,28804,2045328_2045333_2045455,00.html (accessed April 2012).

[106]David D. Kirkpatrick, "Egypt Military Aims to Cement Muscular Role in Government," *New York Times*, July 16, 2011, http://www.nytimes.com/2011/07/17/world/middleeast/17egypt.html?_r=1 (accessed April 2012).

in the wake of a popular uprising remains an unknown, North Korean security forces are certain to play a key role in determining the result of that uprising.

Libya

Libya's military under Gaddafi suffered greatly from the Soviet collapse. Under Gaddafi, the Libyan military consisted of three branches of service: Libyan ground forces, naval forces, and air forces. For much of Gaddafi's reign, he used the military to threaten his neighbors and Israel, but by 2011, it operated with outdated Soviet military equipment than in the days of Soviet support. Following the loss of support from the Soviet Union, UN sanctions limited Gaddafi's ability to modernize his military.

At the start of demonstrations against his government, in the spring of 2011, Gaddafi used his military forces to attack rebel groups in the eastern Libyan cities of Benghazi and Misrata. The biggest advantage in favor of pro-Gaddafi Libyan forces was airpower, against which the rebel groups could not defend. NATO intervened in Libya following the passage of UN Resolution 1973, which provided the mandate to impose a "no-fly" zone against Libyan military aviation and prevent shelling by Libyan ground forces against Libyan citizens.[107] Libyan rebel groups had called for Western intervention to halt air strikes that were causing heavy losses amongst their ranks. NATO intervention reversed the momentum and ultimately led to Gaddafi's demise.

Libya's military varied greatly in capabilities from, elite and loyal brigades to the conscripted and tribal units that eventually joined the rebels' efforts. Gaddafi initially

---

[107]Ademola Abass, "Assessing Nato's Involvement in Libya," United Nations University, October 27, 2011, http://unu.edu/articles/peace-security-human-rights/assessing-nato-s-involvement-in-libya (accessed April 2012).

controlled an estimated four elite brigades totaling approximately 10,000 soldiers. Some of these units were primarily comprised of troops from the same tribe as Gaddafi and were commanded by his sons. One Italian analyst believes Gaddafi had recently been keeping the majority of the army weak and incapable of resisting military action against his regime.[108] Syria based author on Arab affairs Salama Kayla observed that Libyan Army was, "marginalized, and therefore was quick to join the uprising."[109]

Kori Schake, in her article "Lessons of the Libya War," argues that part of the reason NATO considered intervention in Libya a worthwhile endeavor was the limited capability of the Libyan armed forces supporting Gaddafi and the attendant likelihood of NATO success. Schake also asserts that the intervention in Libya sends a dangerous message to anti-government forces in Syria, who may expect NATO involvement in their cause as well.[110] Intervention in the situation in Syria, however, is less likely for several reasons.

Syria

The Syrian military of approximately 330,000 soldiers is currently waging an intense battle against anti-government elements, primarily the FSA, in and around the city of Homs. Syrian military units rely on Russian-made equipment. According to one

---

[108]Sylvia Poggioli, "Gadhafi's Military Muscle Concentrated in Elite Units," National Public Radio, http://www.npr.org/2011/03/10/134404618/gadhafis-military-muscle-concentrated-in-elite-units (accessed May 21, 2012).

[109]Salama Kayla, "Syria's Scenario: Libya or Egypt?" alakbhar english, http://english.al-akhbar.com/content/syria%E2%80%99s-scenario-libya-or-egypt (accessed May 21, 2012).

[110]Schake, "Lessons of the Libya War."

report, Syria is one of the five largest customers for Russian-made military equipment annually. In 2010, Syria purchased nearly six percent of all Russian arms sold that year, including modern T-72 tanks and surface to air missiles.[111] At the order of then ruler Hafez Al-Assad, Syrian security services previously put down a 1982 uprising led by the Muslim Brotherhood. Like his father, Bashar Al-Assad apparently believes that he can also retain power through the use of force.

While Libyan air defenses did not threaten NATO war planes, the Syrian air defense system is integrated and modern. According to U.S. Defense officials quoted in the *New York Times*, Syrian integrated air defenses include short-range missiles, radars, and communication sites located in close proximity to civilian sites.[112] These defenses make NATO or U.S. military involvement more difficult than it had been in Libya. Further, Syrian military forces have received assistance from Iranian military forces and Hezbollah-trained Lebanese militants and, according to a Syrian Army defector serving in the FSA, an Iranian Revolutionary Guard Armored Brigade. Additionally, Hezbollah fighters, such as snipers, explosive experts, and trainers in guerilla warfare, are fighting

---

[111]Dmitry Gorenburg, "Russia Fears Demonstration Effects of Syrian Uprising," Russian Military Word Press, entry posted April 25, 2012, http://russiamil.word press.com/2012/04/25/russia-fears-demonstration-effects-of-syrian-uprising/(accessed May 22, 2012).

[112]Elisabeth Bumiller, "Military Points to Risks of a Syrian Intervention," *New York Times*, March 11, 2012, http://www.nytimes.com/2012/03/12/world/middleeast/us-syria-intervention-would-be-risky-pentagon-officials-say.html? (accessed April 2012).

alongside the Syrian army.[113] These factors add up to a formidable military presence in Syria, which means that the Syrian protesters face a daunting task.

Military defections were significant in the Libyan uprisings. Likewise, some military personnel have defected during the Syrian conflict, but they have not done so in numbers sufficient to tip the balance in the favor of the anti-government forces. It is difficult for conscripted soldiers to defect, because they are generally conscripted out of poverty and poorly, leaving them with no options to support themselves or their families outside of the military. Members of the Alawite sect of Islam comprise the majority of the military's officer corps. The Alawis, the largest religious minority in Syria, have retained power since Hafez Al-Assad became the President in 1971. While Alawis dominate the officer corps, conscripted Sunni troops make up the bulk of the lower ranks. Additionally, objecting soldiers and their families are treated harshly–or even killed. Martin Chulov, in an article in the *The Guardian*, reported the story of one Syrian unit, told they were being sent to fight armed terrorist groups. When the soldiers arrived, commanders ordered them to fire on unarmed civilians. When one soldier objected, he was found dead the next day.[114] Another interviewed Syrian Army soldier said, "I would defect tomorrow if you could protect my family, but if I defected they would arrest my father and my brothers and the whole family would have no income. The regime is still in

---

[113] Amr Ahmed, "Iranian Revolutionary Guard and Hezbollah Aiding Al-Assad in Syria–Fsa Commander," *Asharq Alaswat*, January 3, 2012, http://www.asharq-e.com/news.asp?section=1&id=28677 (accessed April 2012).

[114] Martin Chulov, "Syrian Army Defector Says He Was Told to Shoot Unarmed Protesters," *Guardian*, June 27, 2011, http://www.guardian.co.uk/world/2011/jun/27/syrian-army-defector-wasid-deraa (accessed April 2012).

control."[115] Syria's treatment of defectors resembles North Korea's "three-generation policy," which dictates that three generations of family members are arrested and jailed for political dissent towards the Kim regime. These policies strike fear in families and intimidate opponents.

Unlike Egyptian military leaders who chose to side with the demonstrators to preserve–and perhaps increase–their role in society, the Syrian military, led by Alawite officers, has chosen to side with the regime to preserve its place in Syrian society. The common thread of each country, though, involves a powerful military acting to preserve its status. Both Egypt and Syria, the choices made by the military establishment play a critical role in the success or failure of popular uprisings. Given how dominant the North Korean military is in its society, it is very likely that its choices would have the same impact on any North Korean uprising.

North Korea

The Korean People's Army is responsible for internal security as well as defense of the nation. The Korean People's Army enjoys great status in the Democratic People's Republic of Korea thanks to the policy of Songun, or "military-first" politics, which was established in 1997. While placing the military as the central institution in the creation of domestic and foreign policy is not an entirely new idea, Songun formalized the concept. Those reforms "shifted the locus of political power in North Korea to the Korean People's Army."[116] The Seoul-based Korea Economic Research Institute reported in

---

[115]Joseph Holiday, *Syria's Armed Opposition* (Washington, DC: Institute for the Study of War, 2012), 14.

[116]Holiday, 14; Lind, "Pyongyang Survival Guide," 62.

2011 that North Korea maintains an army estimated to be at one million soldiers.[117] Of those, it is believed 80 percent are deployed within 100 kilometers of the demilitarized zone bordering South Korea. Most of these forces are outfitted with aging Soviet equipment, but they still pose a deadly threat to the large population in Seoul.

The North Korean military functions in a manner comparable to the Egyptian Army, and has created a unique role for itself in everyday life. Like the Egyptian military, the Korean People's Army receives a disproportionate amount of the annual budget and is utilized in domestic roles such as agriculture and construction. Reported wide spread food shortages and famine have not caused the North Korean leaders to alter their military-first policy. On February 18, 2001, North Korean state television broadcast a message from Kim Jong II justifying the need for Songun: "If I would put the first priority on the economy, more fabric will be made and the quality of life of people may become a little better. However, for a while yet, I cannot endanger our·socialist country, forged through blood and fire, for the goal of stuffing our mouths."[118] Kim Jong II created a system that all but guaranteed the loyalty of his military leaders. Yet to be seen, is whether these leaders will give the same support to the younger Kim.

Even when North Korean economic reforms have failed, military members have still benefitted. In November 2009 during the attempted revaluation of its currency, North

---

[117]Jeremy Laurence, "North Korea Military Has an Edge Over South, but Wouldn't Win a War, Study Finds," *Christian Science Monitor*, January 4, 2012, http://www.csmonitor.com/World/Latest-News-Wires/2012/0104/North-Korea-military-has-an-edge-over-South-but-wouldn-t-win-a-war-study-finds (accessed March 2012).

[118]Young Sun Lee and Deok Ryong Yoon, *The Structure of North Korea's Political Economy: Changes and Effects* (Washington, DC: Korea Economic Institute, 2004), 53.

Korea ordered the exchange of old currency for new currency at a rate of 100 to 1. Buying power for regular North Korean citizens collapsed. At the same time, the regime continued to pay government workers, and more importantly military members, at the pre-currency reform levels, basically increasing their purchasing power.[119] North Korea continues to make the military the largest and strongest of its elements of national power, even at the detriment of its economy, largely because its leaders believe the military can insulate the regime from internal and external threats.

"The Network"

To illustrate the dynamic that social networking has brought to the revolutions occurring throughout the Middle East, consider the internet account of a Syrian activist that was stopped at a Syrian military checkpoint and questioned about a "thumb drive" and laptop computer present in the car. The Syrian soldier inspected the items and asked the activist, "Do you have a Facebook?" The activist replied that he did not, and was therefore allowed to pass through the checkpoint.[120] The story highlights the injection of social media into the Arab Spring and the uneven understanding of these new devices across the Middle East. Clearly, Twitter, Facebook, and YouTube have played a significant role in igniting and perpetuating the revolutions and uprisings that occurred throughout the region in 2011. These tools, which connect citizens all around the world, are commonly referred to as information communication technologies or social media

---

[119]Sang Hun Choe, "Economic Measures by North Korea Prompt New Hardships and Unrest," *New York Times*, February 3, 2010, http://www.nytimes.com/2010/02/04/world/asia/04korea.html?_r=1 (accessed April 2012).

[120]Friedman, "If Syria Blows Up."

networks, among other monikers.[121] While these relatively new technologies certainly impacted the Arab Spring, the term The Network, as used here, encompasses additional facets such as organization of opposition groups and reactions by Arab governments to combat the growing demonstrations and their use of social media tools.

Opponents relied on social media networks for internal and external functions in each of the nations where Arab Spring uprisings occurred. Protestors used social media to organize opposition, alert demonstrators to the locations of security forces, and provoke outrage in neighboring countries through the dissemination and broadcasting of violent images and videos. However, it should be remembered that protests and revolutions have occurred throughout history and therefore are possible without social media. For example, the famous Iranian Revolution of 1979 that overthrew the Shah of Iran occurred without the use of social-media networks. So, it has been possible in the past to rally and organize dissent against the governing establishment. However, these modern devices undeniably contributed to the speed of the revolutions and the series of uprisings that occurred throughout the region.

A group of University of Washington researchers recently published a report entitled *Opening Closed Regimes: What was the Role of Social Media During the Arab Spring?* The study analyzes the role technology played during the revolutions. The report draws three conclusions: (1) social media played a central role in shaping political debates in the Arab Spring; (2) spikes in online revolutionary conversations often preceded major events on the ground; and (3) social media helped spread democratic

---

[121]In this paper, the terms social media and information communication technologies will be used interchangeably.

ideas across international borders.[122] These modern informational technology devices were not the sole cause of political discontent in Egypt, Libya, and Syria. However, these instruments helped funnel discontent towards the regimes, organize the tactics of the opposition, and fuel discontent in neighboring countries.

Egypt

For years, Egypt unsuccessfully attempted to suppress political opposition groups from circulating anti-governmental literature. The "6 April Youth Movement" and The Muslim Brotherhood are two of the largest more politically active opposition groups inside Egypt. Shortly after Egyptian citizens began occupying the streets of Cairo, both organizations capitalized on two major factors to rally and organize public opposition to the Mubarak government. Egypt's population is young, largely comfortable with modern technology, and overwhelmingly under-or unemployed. Indeed, the median age of the Egyptian population is just 24 years old, and 70 percent of internet users in Egypt are under the age of 34. Moreover, Egypt has 67 cell phones for every 100 people.[123] Interestingly, according to the Egyptian Ministry of Communications and Information Technology, between the year 2000 and February 2010, internet use in Egypt rose 3,691 percent.[124] Therefore, Mubarak's Egypt had a large population of frustrated, educated,

---

[122]Philip N. Howard, *Opening Closed Regimes?: What Was the Role of Social Media During the Arab Spring?* (Seattle, WA: University of Washington, 2012), 2-4.

[123]Howard, *Opening Closed Regimes*, 5-6.

[124]Ekaterina Stepanova, *The Role of Information Communication Technologies in the "Arab Spring": Implications Beyond the Region* (Washington, DC: George Washington University Elliott School of International Affairs, May 2011), 2.

tech-savvy individuals who could connect to each other through social media and had large amounts of time on their hands.

The, 6 April Youth Movement, was founded by Ahmed Mahed in 2008 on Facebook to rally support for a labor strike in Northern Egypt, a movement that grew in support through the use of social media. Mahed is also credited with planning and organizing the protests that occurred in Cairo following the uprisings in Tunisia. In an interview with *Asharq Alawsat*, an English-language daily newspaper, Mahed said he prepared for the demonstrations by establishing an operations center approximately 15 days before protests began. During these meetings, the youthful organizers would devise innovative ways to share information on social networking sites aimed at countering state security services historical approaches used to pre-empt demonstrations.[125]

Early during the protests, Mubarak ordered the "blackout" of all cell phone, internet and online services. Most of the telecommunications companies adhered to the blackout, but opposition groups were able to discover "work arounds" to stay online. The Muslim Brotherhood, for example, moved its servers to London, outside the reach of Egypt's security and intelligence services. The University of Washington researchers believe the blackout backfired on Mubarak, as the complete shutdown of these services affected regular Egyptian citizens more than protesters and may have bolstered the ranks of Egyptians calling for changes in leadership.[126]

---

[125]Essam Fadl, "Asharq Al-Awsat Talks Egypt's April 6 Youth Movement Founder Ahmed Maher," *Asharq Al-Awsat*, October 2, 2011, http://asharq-e.com/news.asp?section=3&id=24109 (accessed April 2012).

[126]Howard, *Opening Closed Regimes*, 16.

Libya

Unlike the Egyptian citizenry, Libyans are not as advanced in employing modern technology. According to a 2010 World Bank report, only 5.7 percent of Libya's population uses the internet, largely because of a lack of modern infrastructure throughout the country, particularly outside of Tripoli.[127] With so few online users and the lack of a reliable internet infrastructure, Libyan opposition groups struggled initially to communicate with followers and provide information about Libyan security forces to its fighters. Like Mubarak, Gaddafi ordered a blackout for cell phone services. Without cell phone capability, anti-government militias used colored flags to signal orders to their fighters. Later, when the owner of the largest telecommunications company in Libya threw his support behind the rebels, he moved the cell towers from Tripoli (under Gaddafi's control) to cities controlled by the rebels. This move allowed them to communicate much more effectively.[128]

Another aspect that was initially distinctive to the Libyan uprisings was the violence that Libyan security forces used against demonstrators and rebel militias. It is difficult to quantify the levels of violence in each of the Arab Spring revolutions, but it is reasonable to assess that Libya and Syria have seen the longest and most consistent military engagements, against both anti-government groups and civilians. Rebel groups successfully documented the brutal tactics used by Libyan security forces and shared

---

[127] World Bank, "Internet Users as Percentage of Population," Google, Last updated March 30, 2012, http://www.google.com/publicdata/explore?ds=d5bncppjof8f9_ &met_y=it_net_user_p2&idim=country: LBY (accessed April 2012).

[128] Doug Aamoth, "How Libyan Rebels Built Their Own Cellphone Network," *Time*, April 13, 2011, http://techland.time.com/2011/04/13/how-libyan-rebels-built-their-own-cellphone-network/ (accessed April 2012).

these images with the rest of the world through social media and reporters embedded with rebel groups. Gaddafi's refusal to halt the siege by his security forces well into April 2011 played a role in NATO's decision to intervene. Gada Mahfud wrote in the new independent Libyan daily newspaper, the Libyan Herald, that images and videos posted on Facebook and YouTube mobilized public opinion and ultimately pushed NATO and the UN to take action.[129]

Numerous rebel militias around the eastern cities of Benghazi and Misrata formed the Libyan opposition. These forces united to oppose Gaddafi's rule and formed the Transitional National Council, managed by Mustafa Abdel Jalil, a former Justice Minister who defected from the Gaddafi administration. In July 2011, the U.S. recognized the Transitional National Council as the rightful leaders of Libya. The strength of the Libyan rebel groups was their ability to bond together against a common enemy. Tribal affiliations and allegiances did not initially prevent the formation of the Transitional National Council. Additionally, the rebels were quick learners of military tactics with the assistance of NATO mentors. Thus far, Libyan rebels are the only armed opposition groups to successfully overthrow their ruling government with the use of violence. Of course, NATO intervention is likely the largest variable which is only present in Libya. While NATO felt called to act in the case of Libya, the same has not been true for the Syrian situation. U.S. Senator Bob Corker, the second highest ranking member of the Senate Foreign Relations Committee, stated that the Syrian opposition groups are not as organized as the groups in Libya. Corker also feels that the intentions of the Syrian

---

[129]Gada Mahfud, "Opinion: Arab Awakening and Social Media," *Libya Herald*, May 5, 2012, www.libyaherald.com/opinion-the-arab-awakening-social-media (accessed May 2012).

opposition may not be as 'democratic' as was the case in Libya. Corker stated, "I don't think this is near to the place where the opposition was in Libya."[130]

Syria

Former U.S. Army Intelligence Officer Joseph Holliday, in a research study of the Syrian opposition titled *Syria's Armed Opposition*, analyzes the various factions that exist inside Syria and neighboring Turkey. In the report, Holliday concludes that the FSA, headquartered across the Turkish border, has been able to unify to some degree the three largest militias fighting the Al-Assad regime because the Khalid bin Walid Brigade, the Harmoush Battalion, and the Omari Battalion each has pledged allegiance to the FSA. While Holliday surmises that the individual militias are capable fighters who have displayed great resilience, the FSA has been unable to operationalize the relationships. Some significant concerns exist, such as resupplying the militias, but even more important is the inability, thus far, to persuade nations that support the removal of Bashar Al-Assad to arm these rebel organizations.[131]

Sunni citizens from the Eastern provinces of Syria comprise the vast majority of the Syrian opposition. Individual militias have been able to inflict casualties on Syrian security forces while preserving pockets of territory from which to operate. Secretary Panetta recently told the House Armed Services Committee that the U.S. was concerned about the lack of organization amongst the opposition, which deters the U.S. from

---

[130]Josh Rogin, "Senior Republican Senator: Syrian Revolution Not Really About 'democracy'," *Foreign Policy*, http://thecable.foreignpolicy.com/posts/2012/03/13/senior_republican_senator_syrian_revolution_not_really_about_democracy (accessed May 22, 2012).

[131]Holliday, Syria's Armed Opposition, 7.

committing arms to these organizations. Holliday points out in his study that members of Al-Qaeda and other extremist organizations also seek to remove Al-Assad from power.[132] Their involvement likely will further jeopardize American material support to the Syrian opposition.

Like the Egyptian and Libyan opposition before them, the Syrian opposition uses modern social media to organize resistance and publicize the bloodshed inflicted by the Syrian military. Unlike those nations, however, the Syrian government actively monitors the sites that are most widely used to organize protests, such as Facebook and Twitter. Syrian security forces have used that information to identify the locations of demonstrations and crack down on protesters. The Syrian secret police have also been able to identify users on these sites and make arrests. Additionally, Bashar Al-Assad encourages supporters of his regime to make posts and entries on Facebook to show support for his Syrian government. For the first time, both anti-government groups and the regime are using social media in an information war. Interestingly, a 21-year old anti-government activist noted that "The government reopened Facebook because they realized that it was more useful for them to allow activists to communicate on the site, and then track us down using their team of loyalists who search the Internet."[133]

---

[132]Ibid., 35.

[133]Author Anonymous for safety, "Social Media: A Double-Edged Sword in Syria," *Reuters*, http://www.reuters.com/article/2011/07/13/us-syria-social-media-idUSTRE76C3DB20110713 (accessed April 2012).

North Korea

Following the popular uprisings in the Middle East and North Africa, non-profit organizations released balloons into North Korea containing leaflets describing the Arab Spring. The North Korean government responded that the release of the balloons constituted "psychological warfare" by South Korea and would be met by an attack if it continued.[134] In 2011, protests from Tunisia spread to Egypt, Libya, Yemen, Syria, and Bahrain via modern technology and social media sites operated by regular citizens. News of these global affairs literally drifted to North Korean citizens by way of balloons. This phenomenon demonstrates the large gap between information flow in North Korea and the rest of the world.

One North Korean concept which is used to justify this strict control of the population's lives is *Juche*. Juche is commonly translated as "self-reliance". The first time the concept was referenced was a speech given by Kim II Sung to the leaders of the Korean Worker's Party in 1955. However, the meaning of juche that Kim referred to was not the ideology that it has become. Juche is a combination of Chinese and Korean word that means 'subject' or 'one's own identity'. Kim II Sung meant to convey the idea that North Koreans must assert their own identity separate from foreign pressure, likely meaning the Chinese communist movement.[135] Soviet and Chinese communist

---

[134]Wendy Zuckerman, "Balloon Launches Breach North Korea's Bubble," *New Scientist*, March 1, 2011, http://www.newscientist.com/article/dn20180-balloon-launches-breach-north-koreas-bubble.html (accessed March 2012).

[135]Andrei Lankov, "Juche (self-Reliance) On Translation," *Korea Times*, August 26, 2007, http://www.koreatimes.co.kr/www/news/opinon/opi_view.asp?newsIdx=9008&categoryCode=166 (accessed March 2012).

governments put pressure on North Korea to adopt similar types of Marxist-Leninist communist systems. Kim Il Sung wanted North Korea to adopt a system that was true to North Korean values. Over the years, juche has evolved into its current form as North Korea stepped away from the international community. To prove the success of the juche policy to its citizens, North Korea juxtaposes its situation against that of South Korea. "The North Korean narrative depicts South Koreans as contaminated by association with the impure America and as juche's mirror image–servile flunkeys to American masters."[136] Of course it is nearly impossible for the average North Korean to conduct a comparison with their South Korean counterparts.

The largest theme of the juche philosophy is the nationalistic component. Andrew Lankov, a leading scholar on North Korea affairs has argued that the "self-reliance" definition has evolved over the years. His belief is that "self-reliance" was not ever intended to be the meaning of juche. However, Kim Il Sung and later Kim Jong Il used the strict loyalty to the North Korean state behind the juche ideology as a way to garner support for all governmental, economic and military policies. Lankov wrote, "it has much greater connotations with nationalism, and in later years when economic self-reliance, once much trumpeted in Pyongyang, went out of fashion, the nationalistic essence of juche became even more visible."[137]

Kim Il Sung and Kim Jong Il have created a society that strictly controls information to its people. The system is much more complex than just the lack of internet use or the monitoring of cell phone calls. The common perception is that North Korea is

---

[136]Bynum and Lind, *Pyongyang survival guide*, 54.

[137]Lankov, Juche (Self-reliance) on Translation.

the most isolated country in the world in terms of the freedom of information to its people. The physical make-up of North Korea provides the first real sense of the regime insulating itself from internal threats. Residents who live in Pyongyang are granted special permission to live in the city limits. The Pyongyang population consists of the North Korean elite. Residents receive special housing and food rations well above what rural residents receive. This "special class" of North Koreans is afforded better housing and access to "luxuries," such as leather shoes and watches.[138] The approximately 2.5 million residents of Pyongyang have special identification cards that allow them to travel more freely than other North Korean citizens. According to the South Korean Unification Ministry, approximately only 2 percent of defectors are from Pyongyang.[139] The ministry reported over 10,000 defections from North Korea in the period of 2007 to 2010.[140]

Conversely, residents outside the capital are formed into villages, called *inminbans*, normally comprised of 30 to 50 families, totaling about 100 people. The regime assigns a Korean Worker's Party-appointed observer that monitors the residents of those villages to ensure they remain loyal to the state.[141] The North Korean National Security Agency is tasked with monitoring the lives of its population and investigates crimes against the regime. Disapproving any part of the North Korean government can be

---

[138]Ibid.; Lind, "Pyongyang Survival Guide," 62.

[139]*The Chosun Ilbo,* Defectors Skeptical about North Koreans' Grief, *Chosun Ilbo* (English Edition), December 2011, http://english.chosun.com/site/data/html_dir/ 2011/12/22/2011122201543.html (accessed April 2012).

[140]Roger Yu, "Defections on Rise in North Korea," *USA Today*, November 16, 2010, http://www.usatoday.com/news/world/2010-11-16-koreas16_ST_N.htm (accessed May 2012).

[141]Ibid.; Lind, "Pyongyang Survival Guide," 57.

cause for arrest and isolation in a political prison camp.[142] The regime strengthens fear

amongst its people by implementing *yeon-jwa-je* [Korean word], which translates as

"guilt by association." The regime's policy is commonly referred to as, "three generation

policy." Under this policy, the regime has jailed political dissidents and up to three

generations of family members to ensure discontent does not grow.[143] The U.S.'

government estimates there are approximately 200,000 North Koreans imprisoned in the

political prison camps.[144]

Social media sites such as Twitter and Facebook received much of the credit for

the growth and success of the Arab Spring revolutions. One requirement for the use of

these devices is internet service with tech savvy individuals to be able to share

information and thoughts. Estimates put the use of the internet by North Korean citizens

at no more than a couple thousand users.[145] The lack of users would seem to indicate that

the system is not that widely distributed and few North Koreans know how to operate in a

globally connected world. However, Jane Kim from Johns Hopkins School for Advanced

---

[142]Gang Min Nam, "What Kind of Organization Is North Korea's National Security Agency?" *Daily North Korea*, http://www.dailynk.com/english/read.php?catald=nk00400&num=2645 (accessed April 2012).

[143]Robert Park, "North Korea: The World's Principal Violator of the 'responsibility to Protect'," *Columbia Journal of International Affairs* (February 2012), http://jia.sipa.columbia.edu/north-korea-world%E2%80%99s-principal-violator-%E2%80%9Cresponsibility-protect%E2%80%9D (accessed March 2012).

[144]Blaine Harden, "How One Man Escaped from a North Korean Prison Camp," *Guardian*, March 16, 2012, http://www.guardian.co.uk/books/2012/mar/16/escape-north-korea-prison-camp (accessed April 2012).

[145]Martyn Williams, "North Korea Moves Quietly Onto the Internet," *Computerworld*, June 10, 2010, http://www.cio.com/article/596543/North_Korea_Moves_Quietly_Onto_the_Internet?page=2&taxonomyId=3055 (accessed April 2012).

International Studies notes that North Korea has been experimenting with internet use since the late 1990s and has recently connected some government computer systems to the overall global internet. Kim concludes that North Korea intended to use the internet for economic opportunities but thus far has failed or refused to relinquish the control of information.[146] At this time, North Korea lacks sufficient internet distribution or technological knowledge, amongst its people to make the internet a valuable tool for igniting civil resistance.

In North Korea, cell phones are much more widely used than computers or the internet. As of December 2011, approximately one million subscribers use the cell phone network built by Orascom, an Egyptian telecommunications company that was contracted to build the most recent cell phone network in North Korea.[147] Peter Nesbitt of Georgetown University recently argued that North Korean cell services are only prominent among key elites who are unyieldingly loyal to the regime and military members. In fact, he suggests that the increased availability of the cell phone network, may increase North Korea's monitoring of its citizens and even use as a military communication tool to make up for aging radio equipment. The North Korean regime

---

[146]Jane Kim, "Selling North Korea in New Frontiers: Profit and Revolution in Cyberspace," *U.S.-Korea Academic Studies: Emerging Voices* 22 (2011, special edition): 20, http://www.keia.org/sites/default/files/publications/ emergingvoices_final_ janekim.pdf (accessed April 2012).

[147]Kedar Pavgi, "North Korea: Please Turn Off Your Cell Phone... Or Else," *Foreign Policy*, January 27, 2012, http://blog.foreignpolicy.com/posts/2012/01/27/ please_turn_off_all_electronicsforever (accessed March 2012).

was able to completely shut down the cell phone system in 2005 and could again at any point.[148]

The networking factors that existed in Egypt, Libya, and Syria do not currently exist in North Korea. Egypt, Libya, and Syria had established anti-government elements that were able to use modern social networking tools to organize protests and demonstrations against their government leaders. The North Korean system effectively rewards party loyalty, while monitoring and promoting fear amongst its lower classes. The lack of modern technology and knowledgeable users restricts the inflow of external information and the dissemination of internal information. North Korean citizens know only what is given to them by the state and this is one of the larger reasons why a popular uprising is highly unlikely.

---

[148]Peter Nesbitt, "North Koreans Have Cell Phones: Why Cell Phones Won't Lead to Revolution and How They Strengthen the Regime," *U.S.-Korea Academic Studies: Emerging Voices* 22 (2011, special edition): 8-18, http://www.keia.org/sites/default/files/publications/emergingvoices_final_peternesbitt. pdf (accessed April 2012).

CHAPTER 5

CONCLUSIONS

<u>Themes</u>

The examination of the three criteria–(1) geo-political environment, (2) role of the

military in society, and (3) The Network–reveals some common trends among the

disparate Arab Spring revolutions. First, the decision to act (or not act) by foreign nations

significantly impacted the success of the Arab Spring revolutions. As uprisings continue,

global powers such as the U.S., Russia, and China have been forced into deciding

whether to take action or let the protests run their course, based on their national interests.

These decisions have been–and will continue to be–critical to the success or failure of the

Libyan and Syrian revolutions with NATO's intervention in Libya crucial to the ouster of

Moammar Gaddafi and China and Russia's veto of sanctions against Syria serving to

strengthen the Al-Assad's regime.

Secondly, the actions taken by the military in Egypt and Syria–although

divergent–have proven vital to the outcomes of the uprisings in those respective nations.

In Egypt, the military chose to protect its elevated role in society by supporting the

resignation of Hosni Mubarak. By permitting the protests, the military fortified its

position in Egypt and is now overseeing the creation of a new constitution that will

provide for its continued role in in civil-society. Conversely, the Syrian military, led by a

mostly Alawi officer corps, has continued its support for fellow Alawi, Bashar Al-Assad.

Thus, the ruling minority is waging a violent offensive against the Sunni-majority armed

opposition and civilian demonstrators. Bashar Al-Assad can only retain his rule with the

support of the Syrian security forces.

Finally, the ability of people to form networks to pressure their ruling governments is clearly crucial to the Arab Spring. Within Egypt, Libya, and Syria, anti-government opposition groups existed to various degrees prior to their respective revolutions. Some, like those in Egypt, were more organized, but each had an organizational structure that opposed their respective leaders. Once protests began to spread, the opposition groups were able to mobilize support and organize the movement through the use of social media tools. Protesters relied on cell phones, Twitter, Facebook, and YouTube to rally public opinion to their cause, report on government security forces' locations and actions, and ultimately disseminate images of violence to the rest of the world. Although Tunisian street vendor Mohamad Bouazizi may have sparked the Arab Spring through his act of self-immolation, The Network was responsible for spreading the movement and was ultimately critical to its success.

B. R. Myers recently wrote a book titled *The Cleanest Race: How North Korea Sees Itself,* in which, he suggests one of the biggest problems with analyzing North Korea has been the stale opposing viewpoints that analysts of North Korea traditionally have held. He argues that conservatives often describe the North Korean regime actions in terms of survival and trying to hold on to power, while liberal analysts portray the Democratic People's Republic of Korea as "rational actors" who are forced to do what they do because of immense pressure from the U.S. and the West. Myers believes that North Korean people, like their government, strongly believe in the ideology of North

Korea. He believes it is more than just *Juche*, but that it is the ideology that guides the devotion to the North Korean regime and their government's actions.[149]

This study analyzed three criteria to determine the possibility of a popular uprising occurring in North Korea similar to the revolts commonly referred to as the Arab Spring. The criteria were the geo-political environment, the role of the military in society, and The Network, which referred to the ability of the citizens to organize and actually convey their dissatisfaction towards their governments. The *Juche* ideology is so ingrained in the North Korean people that it is hard to fathom that enough citizens would feel vitriolic contempt for Kim Il Sung, Kim Jong Il and now Kim Jong Un. From birth, the North Korean system establishes a serious nationalistic dedication in its citizens. The size and loyalty of its immense national army would make the success of a popular uprising far from likely. North Korea will hold on to its nuclear weapon threat, even more so after the removal of Moammar Gaddafi by NATO following Libya's terminating its nuclear weapons program. Special privilege has been granted to the military that essentially buys their loyalty. Much like in Egypt, the military would seem to want to act in the manner that best maintains their elevated status, and support for the regime accomplishes that goal. The control of information and the lack of modern social networks prevent the "domino effect," which was so prevalent in fueling the Arab Spring revolutions, from happening in North Korea. The seat of power in North Korea, Pyongyang, is surrounded by extremely loyal citizens who would not risk relinquishing

---

[149]B. R. Myers, "'the Cleanest Race'," *New York Times*, January 26, 2010, http://www.nytimes.com/2010/01/28/books/excerpt-cleanest-race.html? pagewanted=all (accessed April 2012).

their elevated status. The analysis indicates that the factors that ignited and powered civil unrest throughout the Middle East and North Africa do not exist in North Korea.

Nevertheless, the North Korean regime is unlikely to be able to repress its people and maintain the status quo forever. The U.S. and its allies must continue to refine its approach to work towards the unification of the Korean peninsula and the human rights of the North Korean people. An important distinction for this study is the difference between popular revolution in North Korea and regime collapse. This study analyzed the possibility of popular revolution to determine its likelihood. While this study concludes that a popular people-led revolution is unlikely, there are other scenarios that end with regime collapse in North Korea, which also presents difficulties for the U.S. and its Asian-Pacific allies. As the North Korean government continues to carry out the transition to Kim Jong Un, a military coup is a possible scenario for regime collapse. Kim Jong Un appears to have the support of the military leaders for now, but incidents such as the failed ballistic missile test in April 2012 could put a strain on that relationship. An article in the *Economist* recently stated, "On the one hand, the lack of reform is leading North Korea down a dead end. On the other, a more open country would surely spell the end of the Kim dynasty."[150] Their assessment is that ultimately the system will fail and that should mean the U.S. and its allies must be more prepared than they were for the events that occurred during the Arab Spring. Kim Jong Un recently gave public remarks during a military celebration in the square in Pyongyang. Kim Jung II had not spoken in public in years and the younger Kim's remarks indicated a willingness to work towards

[150]*The Economist*, "We Need to Talk about Kim," December 31, 2011, http://www.economist.com/node/21542185 (accessed April 2012).

providing for all North Koreans. Future research studies should scrutinize actions by the North Korean government that opens up its society to the world.

The secondary research question that this analysis posed was the existence of a people-led revolutionary model that could provide a scenario similar to the current North Korean situation. One possible model to utilize in searching for ways that the North Korean regime could fall is the Romanian Revolution of 1989. Nicolae Ceausescu ruled Romania from 1965 to 1989 in the manner of the Soviet style communist nations that were concentrated in Eastern Europe during that period. For much of his rule, Ceausescu took its guidance from the Soviet Union and built a similar society. In 1971, Ceausescu visited Pyongyang to meet the then North Korean leader Kim Il Sung. During the visit, the Romanian leader witnessed first-hand the cult of personality that had been built in North Korea that revered Kim Il Sung. Ceausescu was awed by the North Korean nationalistic fervor for communism and the implementation of the *Juche* ideology through systematic education and cultural methods. Following a large earthquake in Bucharest in 1977, Ceausescu set out to build a city much like in Pyongyang.[151] Adam Tolnay of Georgetown University concludes "in all respects Romania in the late 1980s was more akin to North Korea than to Hungary."[152]

A tide of revolution occurred throughout Eastern Europe in 1989 in a very similar way that the Arab Spring struck autocratic-led nations throughout the Middle East.

---

[151]Greg Scarlatoiu, *The Role of the Military in the Fall of the Ceausescu Regime and the Possible Relevance For a Post-Kim Jong-Il Transition in North Korea* (Washington, DC: Korean Economic Institute, 2009).

[152]Adam Tolnay, "Ceausescu's Journey to the East" (diss., Georgetown University), 3, www.ceasescu.org,http://www.ceausescu.org/ceausescu_texts/ TolnayPAPER.pdf (accessed May 14, 2012).

Romania and its neighboring Eastern European communist-style regimes fell in succession, very comparably to the autocratic regimes of Egypt, Yemen, and Libya. Poland, Hungary, Bulgaria, Czechoslovakia, East Germany, and Romania all experienced civil resistance that resulted in those communist regimes being forced from power. In 1989 civil protests occurred in Tiananmen Square in China however it was suppressed successfully by the government. One could conclude that revolutions can have a domino effect, when populations feel they are being unfairly or poorly governed. During 2010 to 2012 there have been very successful, popular revolutions like Egypt, Yemen, and Libya, but also smaller civil protests and demonstrations in places such as Jordan, as well as notable protests of the elections in Russia and even the "Occupy Wall Street" movement throughout American cities. The case could be made that if revolutions continue to spread throughout the world it is not unthinkable that it could make its way to North Korea.

Romania signed the Warsaw Pact in Eastern Europe which bound the nation to the mutual defense of the Soviet Union and its neighboring communist nations. Very much like the China-North Korean relationship, the Union of Soviet Socialist Republics was regarded as sponsors of the Eastern European nations. In fact, during the rule of Leonid Brezhnev the Soviet Union articulated the "Brezhnev Doctrine," which was used to justify military intervention by the Soviet Union to ensure friendly socialist governments were not threatened by the spread of capitalism.[153] However, internal problems began to occur in the Soviet Union throughout the late 1980s. Just prior to becoming the leader of the Soviet Union, Mikael Gorbachev published *Perestroika*, in

---

[153] Adam Roberts, "Civil Resistance in Eastern European and Soviet Revolutions," *The Albert Einstein Institution* 4 (1991): 7, http://www.aeinstein.org/organizations/org/ CivilResistanceintheEastEuropeanandSovietRevolutions.pdf (accessed May 14, 2012).

which he wrote, "The time is ripe for abandoning views on foreign policy which are influenced by an imperial standpoint. Neither the Soviet Union nor the United States is able to force its will on others. It is possible to suppress, compel, bribe, break or blast, but only for a certain period."[154]

The Soviet Union did not intervene in the struggle in Romania. It is not known how China would react to a deteriorating situation in North Korea, but it is not guaranteed they would intervene. This paper has concluded that China historically acts in a manner that is best for their economy and they share immense trade with both South Korea and the U.S.. Major Hak Keun Jin referenced the opinion of Seung Joo Baek, who is a director of the center for security and strategy at Korea Institute for Defense Analyses, "that it is very unlikely for China, considering its relationship with South Korea and the United States, to directly intervene militarily in North Korea as it did during the Korean War."[155]

The divergent actions taken by the militaries in Egypt and Syria suggest that the success or failure of a popular revolution depend largely on the security forces siding with protesters. Romania, during Ceausescu's rule, employed a large military force in addition to the *Securitate*, the large secret police force. Similarly to present day North Korea, political dissent was suppressed quickly, and thus military, police, and the *Securitate* were not accustomed to dealing with large civil protests. Once the protests began, the Romanian military initially attempted to forcefully suppress it by killing dozens of unarmed protestors.

---

[154]Ibid., 8.

[155]Ibid.; Jin, "A Study of China's Possible Military Intervention," 14.

The Romanian Minister of Defense General Vasile Milea was murdered on December 22, 1989. Nicolae Ceausescu promoted his Deputy General Victor Stanculescu to lead the suppression of the protests. However, Stanculescu refused to carry out the order to kill innocent civilians and in fact arrested Ceausescu, who was later tried in a military tribunal and killed by firing squad a few days later.[156] Greg Scarlatoiu, Director of Public Affairs and Business Issues at the Korea Economic Institute wrote, "After the de facto coup by General Stanculescu and the Romanian military ensured the demise of the Ceausescu regime, the military allowed civilian leadership to take control, beginning in the early stages of the transition."[157] Scarlatoiu concludes the military's reasons for not suppressing the protests and in fact arresting, trying, and executing Nicolae Ceausescu was three-fold; (1) the Romanian military believed the role of the military was to support civilian leadership, (2) intense global media pressure would give the Romanian military a negative perception if it replaced one dictatorship for another and, (3) high ranking senior military leaders would receive powerful positions from the newly formed civilian government.[158] The North Korean military, like the Romanian military of 1989, may choose to side with protestors in order to retain power in a coup. Jonathan Levine wrote in *The Atlantic*, "Unless North Korea's generals have bought into the infallibility of the

---

[156]Scarlatoiu, *The Role of the Military in the Fall of the Ceausescu Regime*.

[157]Ibid., 2.

[158]Ibid.

Kim brand it is nothing short of fantastical to assume that this pudgy neophyte will be able to navigate the treacherous straits of Communist Party politics."[159]

While it is unlikely that a Korean Spring is on the horizon, the Romanian Revolution offers a possible model. Just as the Arab Spring took the world by surprise, it is impossible to speak in absolutes about the possibility of a popular uprising in North Korea. Ultimately, this study concludes it is unlikely that an Arab Spring type of revolution is likely in North Korea because of the desire for stability in the geo-political environment, the vast size and status of the North Korean military, and the lack of the modern tools of revolution (Twitter, Facebook, etc). North Korean leaders will do everything in their control to maintain their power. Those expatriated 200 North Korean doctors and nurses should be proof enough.

---

[159]Jonathan Levine, "Will North Korea Attempt a China-Style Opening?" *The Atlantic*, January 17, 2012, http://www.theatlantic.com/international/archive/2012/01/will-north-korea-attempt-a-chinastyle-opening/251493/ (accessed May 14, 2012).

BIBLIOGRAPHY

Published Documents

Bates, Gill. *China's North Korea Policy: Assessing Interests and Influences*. Washington, DC: United States Institute for Peace, July 2011.

Bronson, Rachel. *Saudi Arabia's Intervention in Bahrain*. Philadelphia, PA: Foreign Policy Research Institute, 2011.

Connolly, Michelle, and Kei-Mu Yi. *How Much of South Korea's Growth Miracle Can Be Explained by Trade Policy?* San Francisco, CA: Federal Reserve Bank of San Francisco, September 2008. http://www.frbsf.org/publications/economics/papers/2008/wp08-23bk.pdf (accessed May 20, 2012).

Cordesman, Anthony H. "If Mubarak Leaves: The Role of the Egyptian Military." Center for Strategic and International Studies. February 10, 2011. http://csis.org/publication/if-mubarak-leaves-role-us-military (accessed March 2012).

Cumings, Bruce. *The Korean War: A History*. New York: Random House, Inc., 2010.

Department of Defense. *Sustaining U.S. Global Leadership: Priorities for 21st Century Defense*, Washington, DC: Government Printing Office, 2012.

Gotowicki, LTC Stephan H. *The Military in Egyptian Society*. Washington, DC: National Defense University, 1997.

Harrison, Selig S. *Korean Endgame: A Strategy for Reunification and U.S. Disengagement*. Princeton, NJ: Princeton University Press, 2002.

Holiday, Joseph. *Syria's Armed Opposition*. Washington, DC: Institute for the Study of War, 2012.

Howard, Philip N. *Opening Closed Regimes?: What Was the Role of Social Media During the Arab Spring?* Seattle, WA: University of Washington, 2012.

International Monetary Fund. *World Economic Outlook 2011*. Washington, DC: IMF Multimedia Services Division, 2011.

Kim, Sung Chull, and David Chan-oong Kang, ed. *Engagement with North Korea: A Viable Alternative*. Albany, NY: SUNY Press, 2009.

Korepin, Serge, and Shalini Sharan. *What Does the Arab Spring Mean For Russia, Central Asia and the Caucasus?* Washington, DC: Center for Strategic and International Studies, September 2011.

Kwak, Tae Hwan, and Hong Nack Kim. *Korean Reunification: New Perspectives and Approaches*. Seoul Korea: Kyungnam University Press, 1984.

Lee, Young Sun, and Deok Ryong Yoon. *The Structure of North Korea's Political Economy: Changes and Effects*. Washington, DC: Korea Economic Institute, 2004.

Manyin, Mark E. *U.S.-South Korea Relations*. Washington, DC: Congressional Research Service, November 28, 2011. http://www.fas.org/sgp/crs/row/R41481.pdf (accessed April 2012).

Philip N. Howard. *Opening Closed Regimes?: What Was the Role of Social Media During the Arab Spring?* Seattle, WA: University of Washington, 2012.

Pollack, Jonathan, and Chung Min Lee. *Preparing For Korean Unification: Scenarios and Implications*. Santa Monica, CA: RAND Corporation, 1999. http://www.rand.org/pubs/monograph_reports/2007/MR1040.pdf (accessed January 28, 2011).

Scarlatoiu, Greg. *The Role of the Military in the Fall of the Ceausescu Regime and the Possible Relevance For a Post-Kim Jong-Il Transition in North Korea*. Washington, DC: Korean Economic Institute, 2009.

Schoff, James L., and Yaron Eisenberg. *Peace Regime Building On the Korean Peninsula: What's Next?* Cambridge, MA: Institute for Foreign Policy Affairs, May 2009.

United Nations Security Council. *Resolution 1973*. New York, NY, 2011.

Journals

"Arab Spring Makes North Korea Nervous." *China Post*, November 13, 2011. http://www.chinapost.com.tw/commentary/the-china-post/special-to-the-china-post/2011/11/13/322766/Arab-Spring.htm (accessed May 20, 2012).

Aamoth, Doug. "How Libyan Rebels Built Their Own Cellphone Network." *Time*, April 13, 2011. http://techland.time.com/2011/04/13/how-libyan-rebels-built-their-own-cellphone-network/ (accessed April 2012).

Ajami, Fouad. "America's Alibis for Not Helping Syria." *Hoover Daily Report*, February 24, 2012. http://www.hoover.org/news/daily-report/109346 (accessed April 2012).

———. "Five Myths About the Arab Spring." *Washington Post*, January 12, 2011. http://www.washingtonpost.com/opinions/five-myths-about-the-arab-spring/2011/12/21/gIQA32TVuP_story.html (accessed May 20, 2012).

Anderson, Lisa. "Demystifying the Arab Spring." *Foreign Affairs* (May/June 2011). http://www.foreignaffairs.com/articles/67693/lisa-anderson/demystifying-the-arab-spring (accessed December 7, 2011).

Anonymous. "Social Media: A Double-Edged Sword in Syria." *Reuters*. July 13, 2011. http://www.reuters.com/article/2011/07/13/us-syria-social-media-idUSTRE76C3DB20110713 (accessed April 2012).

Arends, Brett. "IMF Bombshell: Age of America Nears End." *Wall Street Journal*. April 25, 2011. http://www.marketwatch.com/story/imf-bombshell-age-of-america-about-to-end-2011-04-25 (accessed December 20, 2011).

Aronson, Geoffrey. "How the Arab Spring Presages a Shifting World Order." *Foreign Policy*. May 17, 2011. http://mideast.foreignpolicy.com/posts/2011/05/17 how_the_arab_spring_presages_a_shifting_world_order (accessed January 2012).

Bajoria, Jayshree. "The China-North Korea Relationship." *Council on Foreign Relations*, October 7, 2010. http://www.cfr.org/china/china-north-korea-relationship/p11097 (accessed April 2012).

Bar'el, Zvi. "Report: Top Iran Military Official Aiding Assad's Crackdown on Syria Opposition." *Hareetz*. February 6, 2012. http://www.haaretz.com/news/middle-east/report-top-iran-military-official-aiding-assad-s-crackdown-on-syria-opposition-1.411402 (accessed March 2012).

———. "What Exactly Does the U.S. Want from Egypt." *Hareetz*, February 8, 2011. http://www.haaretz.com/print-edition/news/what-exactly-does-the-u-s-want-from-egypt-1.341903 (accessed April 2012).

Beach, Alastair. "Assad Offers an Amnesty to the 'criminals' of the Syrian Uprising." *The Independent*. http://www.independent.co.uk/news/world/middle-east/assad-offers-an-amnesty-to-the-criminals-of-the-syrian-uprising-6290176.html (accessed December 15, 2011).

Bolder, Lolita. "Pentagon Worries Over Chinese Military's Rapid Growth." *Associated Press*, August 25, 2011. http://www.military.com/news/article/pentagon-worries-over-chinese-militarys-rapid-growth.html (accessed December 20, 2011).

Bradley, John R. "Saudi Arabia's Invisible Hand in the Arab Spring." *Foreign Affairs*. October 13, 2011. http://www.foreignaffairs.com/articles/136473/john-r-bradley/saudi-arabias-invisible-hand-in-the-arab-spring (accessed March 2012).

Bumiller, Elisabeth. "Military Points to Risks of a Syrian Intervention." *New York Times*, March 11, 2012. http://www.nytimes.com/2012/03/12/world/middleeast/us-syria-intervention-would-be-risky-pentagon-officials-say.html? (accessed April 2012).

Bynam, Daniel. "Israel's Pessimistic View of the Arab Spring." *Washington Quarterly* 34, no. 3 (2011): 123-36.

Bynum, Daniel, and Jennifer Lind. "Pyongyang's Survival Guide: Tools of Authoritarian Control in North Korea." *International Security* 35, no. 1 (Summer 2010): 44-74.

Cha, Victor. "North Korea's Moment of Truth." *CNN*, December 27, 2011. http://globalpublicsquare.blogs.cnn.com/2011/12/27/cha-north-koreas-moment-of-truth/ (accessed December 2011).

Chae, Kyung-suk. "The Future of the Sunshine Policy: Strategies for Survival." *East-Asian Review* 14, no. 4 (Winter 2002): 2-6. http://www.ieas.or.kr/vol14_4/14_4_1.pdf (accessed April 2012).

Choe, Sang Hun. "Economic Measures by North Korea Prompt New Hardships and Unrest." *New York Times*, February 3, 2010. http://www.nytimes.com/2010/02/04/world/asia/04korea.html?_r=1 (accessed April 2012).

Chulov, Martin. "Syrian Army Defector Says He Was Told to Shoot Unarmed Protesters." *Guardian*, June 27, 2011. http://www.guardian.co.uk/world/2011/jun/27/syrian-army-defector-wasid-deraa (accessed April 2012).

Doughtery, Jill, and Chris Lawrence. "Egypt Warned U.S. Aid at Risk." *CNN*. February 3, 2012. http://security.blogs.cnn.com/2012/02/03/egypt-warned-u-s-aid-at-risk/?hpt=hp_t3 (accessed March 2012).

Elliott, Michael. "Viewpoint: How Libya Became a French and British War Read More." *Time*, March 19, 2011. http://www.time.com/time/world/article/0,8599,2060412,00.html (accessed March 2012).

Freedman, Robert O. "The Arab Spring's Challenge to Moscow." *The Journal of International Security Affairs* 21 (Fall/Winter 2011). http://www.securityaffairs.org/issues/2011/21/freedman.php (accessed March 2012).

Friedman, Thomas. "If Syria Blows Up." *Pittsburgh Post Gazette*. March 30, 2012. http://www.post-gazette.com/stories/opinion/perspectives/thomas-l-friedman-if-syria-blows-up-299069/ (accessed April 2012).

———. "In the Arab World, It's the Past Vs. The Future." *New York Times*, November 26, 2011. http://www.nytimes.com/2011/11/27/opinion/sunday/Friedman-in-the-arab-world-its-the-past-vs-the-future.html?_r=2&ref=opinion (accessed April 28, 2012).

———. "Pray. Hope. Prepare." *New York Times*, April 12, 2011. http://www.nytimes.com/2011/04/13/opinion/13friedman.html (accessed January 2012).

———. "Watching Elephants Fly." *New York Times*, January 7, 2012. http://www.nytimes.com/2012/01/08/opinion/sunday/friedman-watching-elephants-fly.html (accessed December 12, 2011).

Gang Min. "What Kind of Organization Is North Korea's National Security Agency?" *Daily North Korea*. http://www.dailynk.com/english/read.php?catald=nk00400&num=2645 (accessed April 2012).

Gorenburg, Dmitry. "Russia Fears Demonstration Effects of Syrian Uprising." *Russian Military Word Press*. Entry posted April 25, 2012. http://russiamil.word press.com/2012/04/25/russia-fears-demonstration-effects-of-syrian-uprising/ (accessed May 22, 2012).

Habbous, Mahmoud, and Ali Shuaib. "Militias May Drag Libya Into Civil War, Transitional Government Chief Says." *Washington Post*, January 4, 2012. http://www.washingtonpost.com/world/update-1-militias-may-drag-libya-into-civil-war-ntc-chief/2012/01/04/gIQAO8kebP_story.html (accessed January 7, 2012).

Harden, Blaine. "How One Man Escaped from a North Korean Prison Camp." *Guardian*, March 16, 2012. http://www.guardian.co.uk/books/2012/mar/16/escape-north-korea-prison-camp (accessed April 2012).

Hayoun, Massoud. "Coming Arab Identity Crisis-Arab Spring Spurs Hopes For Regional Unity." *The Atlantic*, March 8, 2012.

Hong, Adrian. "How to Free North Koreans." *Foreign Policy*. December 19, 2011. http://www.foreignpolicy.com/articles/2011/12/19/how_to_free_north_korea?page=0,3 (accessed January 2012).

Isachenko, Vladimir. "Russia Backs Assad, Last Friend in Arab World." *Associated Press*, January 29, 2012. http://news.yahoo.com/russia-backs-assad-last-friend-arab-world-101528682.html (accessed April 2012).

Karon, Tony. "Can Syria's Assad Fight His Way to Political Survival?" *Time.com*. February 28, 2012. http://globalspin.blogs.time.com/2012/02/28/syria-can-assad-fight-his-way-to-political-survival/ (accessed April 2012).

———. "Egyptian Military Proving to Be Rival Power Center to Mubarak." *Time*, February 2011. http://www.time.com/time/specials/packages/article/0,28804,2045328_2045333_2045455,00.html (accessed April 2012).

Kelly, Robert. "The German-Korean Unification Parallel." *The Korean Journal of Defense Analysis* 23, no. 4 (December 2011): 461. http://www.kida.re.kr/data/kjda/02_Robert%20Kelly.pdf (accessed January 2012).

Kelly, Suzanne, and Pam Benson. "North Korea's Nuclear Program." *CNN*. December 20, 2011. http://security.blogs.cnn.com/2011/12/20/north-koreas-nuclear-program/ (accessed January 8, 2011).

Kim, Bona. "China's Policy Towards North Korea Redefined." *Daily North Korea*. http://www.dailynk.com/english/read.php?cataId=nk00100&num=5550 (accessed May 2012).

Kim, Jane. "Selling North Korea in New Frontiers: Profit and Revolution in Cyberspace." *U.S.-Korea Academic Studies: Emerging Voices* 22 (2011 Special Edition): 20. http://www.keia.org/sites/default/files/publications/emergingvoices_final_jane kim.pdf (accessed April 2012).

Kramer, Martin. "Syria's Alawis and Shi'ism." http://www.geocities.com/martin kramerorg/Alawis.htm (accessed May 31, 2012).

Landler, Mark. "For Obama, Some Vindication of Approach to War." *New York Times*, October 20, 2011. http://www.nytimes.com/2011/10/21/world/africa/qaddafis-death-is-latest-victory-for-new-us-approach-to-war.html (accessed April 2012).

Lankov, Andrei. "Conditions Unripe For North Korea Revolt." *Asia Times*, November 17, 2011. http://atimes.com/atimes/Korea/MK17Dg01.html (accessed December 2011).

———. "Staying Alive: Why North Korea Will Not Change." *Foreign Affairs* 87, no. 2 (March/April 2008): 15.

Laurence, Jeremy. "North Korea Military Has an Edge Over South, but Wouldn't Win a War, Study Finds." *Christian Science Monitor*, January 4, 2012. http://www.csmonitor.com/World/Latest-News-Wires/2012/0104/North-Korea-military-has-an-edge-over-South-but-wouldn-t-win-a-war-study-finds (accessed March 2012).

Lee, Jean H., and Sam Kim. "Kim Jong Un, North Korea New Leader, Fashions Himself as Reincarnation of Kim II Sung." *Huffington Post*, January 17, 2012. http://www.huffingtonpost.com/2012/01/07/kim-jong-un_n_1191337.html (accessed May 20, 2012).

Levine, Jonathan. "Will North Korea Attempt a China-Style Opening?" *The Atlantic*, January 17, 2012. http://www.theatlantic.com/international/archive/2012/01/will-north-korea-attempt-a-chinastyle-opening/251493/ (accessed May 14, 2012).

Lindsay, James M. "The Globalization of Politics: American Foreign Policy for a New Century." *Brookings Review* (Winter 2003). http://www.cfr.org/world/globalization-politics-american-foreign-policy-new-century/p6330 (accessed May 18, 2012).

Lynch, Marc. "The Big Think Behind the Arab Spring." *Foreign Policy*. November 28, 2011. http://www.foreignpolicy.com/articles/2011/11/28/the_big_think (accessed December 2011).

Mahfud, Gada. "Opinion: Arab Awakening and Social Media." *Libya Herald*, May 5, 2012. www.libyaherald.com/opinion-the-arab-awakening-social-media (accessed May 2012).

Moon, Katharine. "South Korean-U.S. Relations." *Asian Perspective* 28, no. 4 (2004): 42-43. http://www.asianperspective.org/articles/v28n4-c.pdf (accessed April 2012).

Myers, B. R. "Dynasty, North Korean-Style." *New York Times*, January 7, 2012. http://www.nytimes.com/2012/01/08/opinion/sunday/dynasty-north-korean-style.html?_r=1 (accessed January 2012).

————. "'The Cleanest Race'." *New York Times*, January 26, 2010. http://www.ny times.com/2010/01/28/books/excerpt-cleanest-race.html?pagewanted=all (accessed April 2012).

Nesbitt, Peter. "North Korea have Cell Phones." *U.S.-Korea Academic Studies: Emerging Voices* 22 (2011 Special Edition): 8-18. http://www.keia.org/sites/default/files/publications/emergingvoices_final_peternesbitt.pdf (accessed April 2012).

Nixon, Ron. "U.S. Groups Helped Nurture Arab Uprisings." *New York Times*, April 14, 2011. http://www.nytimes.com/2011/04/15/world/15aid.html?_r=1&hp (accessed April 2012).

Obaid, Nawaf. "There Will Be No Uprising in Saudi Arabia." *Foreign Policy*. March 10, 2011. http://www.foreignpolicy.com/articles/2011/03/10/there_will_be_ no_uprising_in_saudi_arabia (accessed December 13, 2011).

Park, Robert. "North Korea: The World's Principal Violator of the 'responsibility to Protect'." *Columbia Journal of International Affairs* (February 2012). http://jia.sipa.columbia.edu/north-korea-world%E2%80%99s-principal-violator-%E2%80%9Cresponsibility-protect%E2%80%9D (accessed March 2012).

Patterson, Eric. "The Arab Spring vs. Cairo." *Foreign Policy Journal,* November 4, 2011. http://www.foreignpolicyjournal.com/2011/11/04/the-arab-spring-vs-cairo/ (accessed December 8, 2011).

Rogin, Josh. "Clinton Confronts the Paradox of America's Role in the Arab Spring." *Foreign Policy*. November 7, 2011. http://thecable.foreignpolicy.com/posts/2011/11/07/clinton_confronts_the_paradox_of_america_s_role_in_the_arab_spring(acc essed March 2012).

————. "Senior Republican Senator: Syrian Revolution Not Really About 'democracy'."
    Foreign Policy. http://thecable.foreignpolicy.com/posts/2012/03/13/
    senior_republican_senator_syrian_revolution_not_really_about_democracy
    (accessed May 22, 2012).

Roy, Denny, PhD. "China and the Korean Peninsula: Beijing's Pyongyang Problem and
    Hope." *Asia-Pacific Security Studies* 3, no. 1 (January 2004): 1-4.
    http://www.apcss.org/Publications/APSSS/ChinaandtheKoreanPeninsula.pdf
    (accessed April 2012).

Salt, Jeremy. "Containing the 'Arab Spring'." *Interface Journal* (May 2012): 54-66.
    http://www.interfacejournal.net/wordpress/wp-content/uploads/2012/05/Interface-
    4-1-Salt.pdf (accessed May 18, 2012).

Schake, Kori. "Lessons of the Libya War." *Defining Ideas*. October 13, 2011.
    http://www.hoover.org/publications/defining-ideas/article/96531 (accessed April
    2012).

Stepanova, Ekaterina. *The Role of Information Communication Technologies in the
    "Arab Spring": Implications Beyond the Region.* Washington, DC: George
    Washington University Elliott School of International Affairs, May 2011.

Takesada, Hideshi. "The Birth of a Unified Korea." *The Brown Journal of World Affairs*
    7, no. 1 (Winter/Spring 2001): 95. http://www.watsoninstitute.org/bjwa/
    archive/8.1/Korea/Takesada.pdf (accessed April 2012).

Yan, Holly. "Why China, Russia Won't Condemn Syrian Regime." *CNN*. February 5,
    2012. http://www.cnn.com/2012/02/05/world/meast/syria-china-russia-
    relations/index.html?hpt=hp_t2 (accessed April 2012).

Yu, Roger. "Defections on Rise in North Korea." *USA Today*, November 16, 2010.
    http://www.usatoday.com/news/world/2010-11-16-koreas16_ST_N.htm (accessed
    May 2012).

Zakaria, Fareed. "Will North Koreans Rise Up?" *CNN*. November 14, 2011.
    http://globalpublicsquare.blogs.cnn.com/2011/11/14/zakaria-will-the-north-
    koreans-rise-up/ (accessed December 12, 2011).

Zuckerman, Wendy. "Balloon Launches Breach North Korea's Bubble." *New Scientist*,
    March 1, 2011. http://www.newscientist.com/article/dn20180-balloon-launches-
    breach-north-koreas-bubble.html (accessed March 2012).

Internet

Abass, Ademola. "Assessing NATO's Involvement in Libya." United Nations University. October 27, 2011. http://unu.edu/articles/peace-security-human-rights/assessing-nato-s-involvement-in-libya (accessed April 26, 2012).

Danin, Robert M. "Remembering Hafez Al-Assad." Council on Foreign Relations: Middle East Matters. Posted November 11, 2011. http://blogs.cfr.org/danin/2011/11/11/remembering-hafez-al-assad/ (accessed March 2011).

East-West Center. "Clinton: America's Future Linked to Future of Asia Pacific Region." http://www.eastwestcenter.org/news-center/east-west-wire/clinton-americas-future-linked-to-future-of-asia-pacific-region (accessed December 17, 2011).

Fadl, Essam. "Asharq Al-Awsat Talks Egypt's April 6 Youth Movement Founder Ahmed Maher." *Asharq Al-Awsat*, October 2, 2011. http://asharq-e.com/news.asp?section=3&id=24109 (accessed April 2012).

Flake, Gordon. "China's Approach to North Korea." The Korea Society. May 5, 2011. http://www.koreasociety.org/policy/policy/chinas_approach_to_north_korea.html (accessed April 2012).

Hornberger, Jacob G. "Egypt's Military Problem." Hornberger's Blog. Entry posted July 18, 2011. http://www.fff.org/blog/jghblog2011-07-18.asp (accessed March 2012).

Kayla, Salama. "Syria's Scenario: Libya or Egypt?" alakbhar english. http://english.al-akhbar.com/content/syria%E2%80%99s-scenario-libya-or-egypt (accessed May 21, 2012).

Kim, John, and Andray Abrahamian. "Why World Should Watch Rason." The Diplomat Blogs. Entry posted December 22, 2011. http://the-diplomat.com/new-leaders-forum/2011/12/22/why-world-should-watch-rason/ (accessed May 20, 2012).

Lacher, Wolfram. "The Libyan Revolution: Old Elites and New Political Forces." *German Institute For International and Security Affairs* 27 (February 2012): 11-14. http://www.swp-berlin.org/fileadmin/contents/products/research_papers/2012_RP06_ass.pdf#page=11 (accessed April 2012).

Pavgi, Kedar. "North Korea: Please Turn Off Your Cell Phone... Or Else." *Foreign Policy*. January 27, 2012. http://blog.foreignpolicy.com/posts/2012/01/27/please_turn_off_all_electronicsforever (accessed March 2012).

Poggioli, Sylvia. "Gadhafi's Military Muscle Concentrated in Elite Units." National Public Radio. http://www.npr.org/2011/03/10/134404618/gadhafis-military-muscle-concentrated-in-elite-units (accessed May 21, 2012).

Roberts, Adam. "Civil Resistance in Eastern European and Soviet Revolutions." *The Albert Einstein Institution* 4 (1991): 7. http://www.aeinstein.org/ organizations/org/CivilResistanceintheEastEuropeanandSovietRevolutions.pdf (accessed May 14, 2012).

The Economist. "The King's Sad Men." May 5, 2012. http://www.economist.com/ node/21554229 (accessed April 2012).

————. "We Need to Talk About Kim." December 31, 2011. http://www.economist.com/node/21542185 (accessed April 2012).

South Korea's Unification Plan. *Spiegel.* March 10, 2012. http://www.spiegel.de/ international/world/0,1518,820577,00.html (accessed April 2012).

The Chosun Ilbo. "Defectors Skeptical about North Koreans' Grief." *Chosun Ilbo* (English Edition), December 2011. http://english.chosun.com/site/data/ html_dir/2011/12/22/2011122201543.html (accessed April 2012).

The White House. Remarks by The President (Barack Obama) "On a New Beginning." Press Release. Cairo, Egypt, 2009.

Walker, Hunter. "Michele Bachmann Blasts Obama for Not 'standing by' Israel and Mubarak." Politicker.com. February 9, 2012. http://politicker.com/2012/02/ 09/michele-bachmann-blasts-obama-for-not-standing-by-israel-and-mubarak/ (accessed May 20, 2012).

Williams, Martyn. "North Korea Moves Quietly Onto the Internet." *Computerworld*, June 10, 2010. http://www.cio.com/article/596543/North_Korea_Moves_ Quietly_Onto_the_Internet?page=2&taxonomyId=3055 (accessed April 2012).

World Bank. "Internet Users as Percentage of Population." Google. Last updated March 30, 2012. http://www.google.com/publicdata/explore?ds=d5bncppjof8f9_& met_y=it_net_user_p2&idim=country:LBY (accessed April 2012).

Zalman, Amy. "Timeline of North Korea's Nuclear Weapons Program." About.com. http://terrorism.about.com/od/usforeignpolicy/a/NorthKorea.htm (accessed January 8, 2011).

Thesis/Dissertation

Jin, Hakkeun. "A Study of China's Possible Military Intervention in the Event of Sudden Change in North Korea." Master's thesis, Command and General Staff College, Fort Leavenworth, KS, 2011. http://cgsc.contentdm.oclc.org/cdm/singleitem/ collection/p4013coll2/id/2784/rec/1 (accessed March 2012).

Tolnay, Adam. "Ceausescu's Journey to the East." diss., Georgetown University. www.ceasescu.org, http://www.ceausescu.org/ceausescu_texts/TolnayPAPER.pdf (accessed May 14, 2012).

www.ingramcontent.com/pod-product-compliance
Lightning Source LLC
Chambersburg PA
CBHW081841280526
45789CB00007B/2523